DICTIONARY
OF
SOUTH AND SOUTHEAST
ASIAN ART

GWYNETH CHATURACHINDA
SUNANDA KRISHNAMURTY
PAULINE W. TABTIANG

SILKWORM BOOKS

ISBN 974-7100-97-5

First published in 2000, reprinted 2001 by
Silkworm Books
104/5 Chiang Mai–Hot Road, M. 7, Suthep, Chiang Mai 50200, Thailand
E-mail: silkworm@loxinfo.co.th

Cover photograph © 1995 by Umaphon Soetphannuk
Photographs © 1995 by Umaphon Soetphannuk
Line drawings by Monticha Khantachawana
Set in 10 pt. Garamond

Printed by O. S. Printing House, Bangkok

01 02 03 04   5 4 3 2

INTRODUCTION

With this work we have endeavored to fill a gap in the dictionaries and glossaries currently available on the history and art of South and Southeast Asia. During the years that we have studied and written on the history and art of the countries of this region, and during the many journeys we have made to these countries, we felt the need for a single volume that would provide concise definitions of the many unfamiliar terms we came across. This dictionary consists of simple explanations, with some illustrations, of the historical, religious, mythological, and architectural terms that the lay person and student are likely to come across when studying subjects related to South and Southeast Asia. We hope it will also prove a useful and easily portable handbook for travelers who visit the historical and religious sites of this region.

We realize there are gaps in this work, but we have tried to include the terms we consider the reader most likely to come across in published works. This dictionary covers a broad base, the terms and their meanings being collected entirely from the publications of scholars who have written on this region. When one word has two different spellings in Sanskrit and Pali, we have defined the Sanskrit word and given a cross-reference for the Pali. For example, *triloka* is the main entry, with a cross-reference for *trailoka*. In English, both *ch* and *c* are used to spell the same Sanskrit sound; likewise for *sh* and *s*. Here, we use *ch* as in Mahavairoc*h*ana and *sh* as in *Sh*iva. In order to maintain a simple format, we have not included diacritics or accents in the transcriptions of Sanskrit and Pali words.

This dictionary is dedicated to our children who appreciate the long history of artistic achievements in this region:

Ravida and *Kamthon*
Parvati and *Arundhati*
Ramon and *Kimberly*

CHRONOLOGY OF SOUTH AND SOUTHEAST ASIA

Before the Common Era (B.C.E.)

1500–1200 B.C.E.	**India** - Vedas **Southeast Asia** - **Thailand**: Ban Chiang culture
800–600	**India** - Upanishads
500	**India** - Mahaparinirvana of the Buddha; year 1 of the Buddhist era and beginning of the historical period
400	**Southeast Asia** - Bronze Age culture - **Vietnam**: Dongson culture (Late Bronze Age)
300	**India** - Alexander the Great reaches India
200	**India** - Reign of King Ashoka - Buddhist missionaries travel to nearby countries
200	**Southeast Asia** - Beginning of Iron Age - First use of lacquer in Vietnam - **Vietnam**: Early historical period - First exchanges with India

100   **Sri Lanka**
- Building of Anuradhapura
- Writing of the Pali Canon

Southeast Asia
- **Vietnam**: Beginning of one thousand years of Chinese occupation

Common Era (C.E.)

0–100   **Southeast Asia**
- Beginning of Indianization; Buddhist monks in Vietnam

100–200   **India**
- Appearance of Greco Buddhist art of Gandhara; art style of Mathura; art style of Amaravati

Southeast Asia
- **Vietnam**: Han style brick tombs; earliest artifacts from Oc-eo

200–300   **Southeast Asia**
- Kingdom of Lin-yi which later becomes northern part of Champa kingdom
- Pyu kingdom of the Irrawaddy

300–400   **India**
- Beginnings of the Gupta era and Gupta art style
- Gandhara art flourishes

Southeast Asia
- Sanskrit inscriptions from Champa

400–500   **India**
- Mahayana Buddhist caves of Ajanta, Ellora
- End of the Gupta dynasty

Southeast Asia
- **Thailand**: Influence of South Indian art

500–600   **India**
- Cave art of Ajanta, Ellora

500–600   **Southeast Asia**
- End of Fu-nan kingdom
- **Cambodia**: Beginnings of Chen-la kingdom
- **Thailand**: Gupta influences in Thai sanctuaries; Khmer inscriptions in eastern provinces

600–700   **India**
- Reign of Mahendravarman I, Pallava dynasty of southeast India.
- Pallava art style.

Southeast Asia
- **Champa**: Mi-Son site established
- **Java**: Beginning of the Shrivijaya kingdom
- **Thailand**: Rise of the Dvaravati school of art; Pre-Angkorian art in the eastern provinces of modern Thailand; Buddhist inscriptions; founding of Haripunjaya kingdom

700–800   **India**
- Pala dynasty in Bengal and Bihar
- Rise of Mahayana and Tantric Buddhism

Southeast Asia
- Indonesian raids in the Indochina peninsula
- **Java**: Sailendra dynasty established
- **Thailand**: Shrivijaya kingdom rules in the peninsula

800–900   **India**
- Chola art

Southeast Asia
- **Cambodia**: Reign of Jayavarman II; reign of Indravarman I; temples founded at Roluos, Prah Ko, Bakong; founding of Angkor
- **Burma**: founding of Pegu
- **Champa**: Buddhist temple of Dong-duong established
- **Thailand**: Mahayana school of Buddhism dominates Shrivijaya; Pallava influences in Peninsula art

900–1000   **India**
- Khajuraho
Southeast Asia
- **Cambodia**: Reign of Jayavarman IV; new capital at Koh Ker
- **Vietnam**: Independence from China
- **Champa**: Invaded by Vietnam

1000–1100   **India**
- Sacking of Buddhist temples of Mathura
Southeast Asia
- **Thailand**: Khmer expansion reaches Lopburi and Menam plain; Angkor art at Lopburi
- **Burma**: Pagan established
- **Cambodia**: Baphuon school of Khmer art

1100–1200   **India**
- Hoysala art
- Sena dynasty in Bengal
Southeast Asia
- **Cambodia**: Founding of Angkor Wat; capture of Angkor by Champa; construction of Angkor Thom, Bayon
- **Thailand**: Expansion of Khmer into Sukhothai

1200–1300   **India**
- Muslim art in Delhi
Southeast Asia
- **Champa**: Annexed by Cambodia
- **Vietnam**: Tran dynasty
- **Burma**: Pagan defeated by Mongols
- **Thailand**: Founding of Sukhothai kingdom; independence of Lopburi; decline of Shrivijaya in peninsula; founding of Chiang Mai as capital of Lan Na kingdom; sculptures in U Thong art syle; Lan Na art style

1300–1400   **India**
- Founding of Vijayanagar

1300–1400	**Southeast Asia**
	- **Vietnam**: Conquers Champa
	- **Peninsula**: Spread of Islam
	- **Laos**: Founding of kingdom of Lan Chang
	- **Burma**: Founding of Ava
	- **Thailand**: Ayutthaya kingdom; Sukhothai school of art flourishes; Sawankalok ceramics; Lan Na kingdom
	- **Champa**: Campaigns against Vietnam
1400–1500	**India**
	- Development of Muslim architecture
	Southeast Asia
	- **Cambodia**: Angkor defeated by Ayutthaya; capital moves to Phnom Phen
	- **Thailand**: Sukhothai subjected by Ayutthaya
1500–1600	**India**
	- Beginning of Mughal empire and architecture; fall of Vijayanagar empire
	Southeast Asia
	- **Burma**: Pegu annexed by Taungu dynasty
	- **Laos**: Capital moved from Luang Prabang to Vientiane
1600–1700	**India**
	- Reign of Shah Jahan
	- Bombay ceded to England
	Southeast Asia
	- **Vietnam**: Divided into two kingdoms under Trinh(north) and Nguyen (south)
	- **Thailand**: Burmese conquer Chiang Mai; Ayutthaya establishes relations with Europe and Japan
	- **Burma**: Ava is capital
	- **Vietnam**: Hue is capital
1700–1800	**India**
	- End of Mughal power

1700–1800   **Southeast Asia**

- **Laos**: Divided into 3 kingdoms
- **Cambodia**: Loses southern provinces to Nguyen dynasty of Vietnam
- **Burma**: Founding of Rangoon
- **Laos**: Vientiane taken by Chao Phraya Chakri of Thailand
- **Vietnam**: Treaty between France and Nguyen dynasty of the south
- **Thailand**: Ayutthaya sacked by Burma; Chakri dynasty established in Bangkok; Wat Phra Kaeo containing the Emerald Buddha was built

1800–1900   **Southeast Asia**

- **Burma**: First Anglo-Burmese war; Ava destroyed by earthquake; founding of Mandalay
- **Cambodia**: Under Vietnam
- **Thailand**: Commercial treaty with East India Company and U.S.; reign of King Rama V, King Chulalongkorn

Nataraja

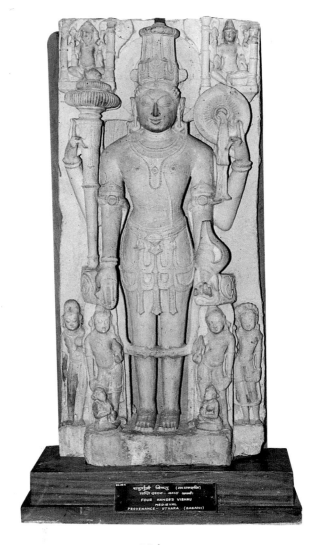

Vishnu

Ganesha

prasat

redented chedi

*bai raka
and chofa*

prang

yoni and linga

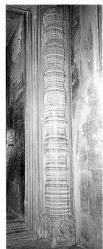

pilaster

Ban Chiang style pottery

niche

bai sema:
four
examples

A

abhayamudra

Hand gesture of a Buddha image represent-ing the dispelling of fear, or the giving of protection. The right hand is held out at chest level, palm outward and the fingers pointing up, usually seen on a standing image. In Thailand the same gesture is also performed with the left hand or both hands. The gesture of raising both hands can be interpreted as calming the ocean.

abhisheka

Ritual unction. The abhisheka of Shri depicts the goddess seated on a lotus, holding a lotus in each hand and doused with water by two elephants. It is a symbol of prosperity in both Buddhist and Hindu iconography.

achara

Rules of ritual practice of religions, orders, and castes.

Adi-Buddha

Adi means first, chief, beginning. The Adi-Buddha is the supreme primordial Buddha in the Vajrayana sect of Mahayana Buddhism who created himself from the original void. The Adi-Buddha is abstract, inconceivable, the true essence which underlies the world of illusion and therefore cannot be revealed in art. However, there are revealed forms in Khmer art, namely Vajradhara and Vajrasattva and various bodhisattvas. In Java, Vairochana is considered to be the Adi-

abhayamudra:
two variations

Buddha. These various revealed forms are usually depicted in princely attire, or in yabyum with a consort.

Agastya

An Indian rishi honored as a scholar of literature and science who appears in the Ramayana and is believed to have brought Hinduism to South India. In Java he is associated with the worship of Shiva.

Agni

The god of fire, often depicted with a ram. Known as the originator of sacrificial rites, Agni was the messenger who linked man with the gods. Agni was one of the three great Vedic gods with Indra and Surya; Agni presided over the earth, Indra over the air, and Surya over the sun and the sky.

ahimsa

Nonviolence in thought, action, and speech according to Buddhist texts.

Airavata

Three-headed elephant, a symbol of the clouds and the vehicle of the god Indra, produced during the churning of the ocean of milk.

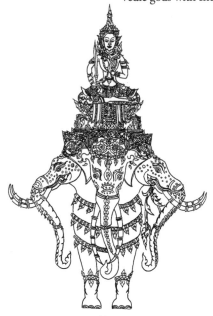

Airavata

Ajanta Caves

Buddhist site dating from 200 B.C.E. to 650 C.E. Twenty-nine man-made caves cut from volcanic rock in a crescent-shaped hillside in West India. Sculptures and murals depict the life of the Buddha. It is a World Heritage site.

Alexander the Great

King of Macedon, Greek conqueror who invaded India in 326 B.C.E. When he left India, Greek artisans settled in North India and possibly influenced the first known anthropoid images of the Buddha, which developed into the Gandhara style of Buddhist art.

am

A small shrine in a Vietnamese temple honoring a Buddhist icon.

amalaka

A circular, ribbed decorative motif at the top of the superstructure of a northern-style Hindu temple.

Amaravati

A site in South India where a Buddhist school of art developed from the 2nd to the

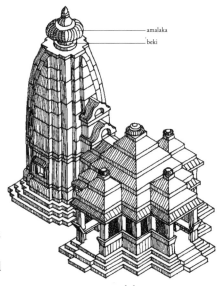

amalaka

4th centuries C.E. Also the capital of Indra's heaven, renowned for its splendor, and situated near the mythical Mt. Meru.

Amareswara

"Lord of the immortals." A title of Vishnu, Shiva, and Indra.

Amitabha

The Buddha of the past and transcendental Buddha of Mahayana Buddhism. He eventually replaced the Shakyamuni Buddha in importance in China and Japan. By calling on him, one can be reborn in paradise and consequently attain Buddhahood in one's next rebirth. He is one of the most popular jinas, and one of his emanations is the Avalokitesvara, who always wears a figure of Amitabha in his headdress. Usually shown seated in meditation.

amrita

The elixir of immortality produced when the gods and demons churn the ocean of milk in the Indian epic poem, the Ramayana. The legend also appears in the Hindu epic, the Mahabharata. It is often identified with soma.

Amritsar

Site of the Golden Temple of the Sikh religion located in the Punjab. Amritsar derives its name from the sacred tank surrounding the temple called amrit, "waters of immortality."

amulet

A protective ornament or charm believed to protect the wearer from misfortune.

Ananda

The Buddha's cousin and his chief disciple. In art, often represented as a young monk with the elderly Kassapa.

Ananta

"Boundless, eternal, infinite." The mythical serpent upon which the Hindu god Vishnu rests during the night that separates two cosmic time periods. The serpent is also known as Shesha.

Anatasayin

The term used for Vishnu when reclining on the back of the coiled serpent, Shesha.

Anawrahta

The forty-second ruler of the Pagan dynasty, ruling from 1044 to 1077 C.E. One of the great kings of Burma who unified the country. A zealous convert to Theravada Buddhism, he was responsible for building many of the pagodas of Pagan; his most famous monument is the Shwezigon pagoda.

Angkor

"City; capital." An ancient capital in Cambodia, the center of the Khmer empire from 802 to 1432 C.E.

Angkor Thom

The great city that was built in the 12th century C.E. by the Khmer king Jayavarman VII. It is located north of Angkor Wat, with the great temple of the Bayon at its center.

Angkor Wat

The largest of the Khmer temples. Built in the early 12th century C.E. by King Surya-varman II, it is dedicated to Vishnu. It is a replica in stone of Khmer cosmology: its five towers symbolize Mt. Meru's five peaks, the enclosing wall represents the mountains at the edge of the world, and the surrounding moat, the oceans beyond.

anicca

The impermanence of all existence, in Buddhism. One of the three characteristics of existence, along with anatta (non ego) and dukha (suffering).

aniconic

Not shaped in human or animal form. For several hundred years after the death of the Buddha, aniconic symbols, such as a bodhi tree, an empty throne, a wheel, a footprint, and a stupa were used to remind the Buddha's followers of his teaching.

animism

The belief that all animate and inanimate things have a soul.

Annam

Former country of Southeast Asia incorporated into Vietnam in 1946 as central Vietnam. Bronze age civilization flourished there when it was conquered by the Chinese in approximately 214 B.C.E. The Chinese named it An Nam, "peaceful south." It became independent in 1428.

antarala

Vestibule or cham-ber in front of a Hindu shrine.

antefix

An upright orna-ment at the lower edge of a roof pro-jecting upwards from the top of a cornice.

apsaras

Female divinities; celestial dancers who are the attendants of Kama, the god of love. The nymphs of Indra's heaven and the companions of the gandharvas. They are able to change shape at will, and are employed by the gods to seduce ascetics.

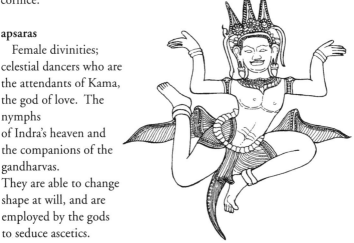

apsara

arahat

In Theravada Buddhism, one who has attained the highest level of spiritual perfection leading to nirvana and is freed from the cycle of rebirth. Revered Buddhist monks are sometimes regarded as arahats;

Ardhanari

images cast of such monks are often placed in temples.

Ardhanari

A composite image of male and female energy depicted as the Hindu god Shiva, with his consort Uma or Parvati. The right side is that of the god and the left is his consort.

arhat

See **arahat**.

Arjuna

Hero of the Indian epic poem, the Mahabharata. Krishna is his charioteer.

Aryan

A group of people who migrated to India from central Asia during the second millennium B.C.E. bringing their own language, culture, and religion. Their rituals and ideas are recorded in the Vedas.

asana

The position of the legs of a god; also a seat or throne.

Ashoka

The Indian emperor who unified India and ruled from approximately 273 to 236 B.C.E. During his reign Buddhism was adopted as the state religion. He erected stone pillars and rock tablets inscribed with Buddhist ethics throughout his empire and sent Buddhist missionaries to many parts of Asia, including Ceylon and Southeast Asia.

ashram

A hermitage retreat for holy men and women.

asura

A demon or demigod who represents the forces of darkness and evil and is constantly at war with the gods.

ashvamedha

Sacrifice of a horse. A sacrifice performed in Vedic times by kings who wanted to dominate their enemies, maintain supremacy, and also produce a male offspring.

Ashwapati

Lord of the horses.

Ashwins

"Horsemen." Two Vedic deities, twin sons of the sky or the sun. They are the personification of early morning light, and said to be the children of a nymph called Ashwini who concealed herself in the form of a mare.

atman

Philosophical concept of universal soul or spirit in Hinduism.

attributes

Particular identifying objects held in the hands of some Hindu gods and goddesses, such as a lotus, a book, a chakra, or a club.

Avalokitesvara

A compassionate male deity in Mahayana Buddhism who delays his own attainment of Buddhahood until he has helped all human-kind to reach that goal. The image of Amitabha is seen in his headdress. His body is sometimes covered with numerous small images of the Buddha. He has many forms with different names; in Southeast Asia he is called Lokesvara and Padmapani. In Khmer art, he carries a rosary, book, flask, and lotus. In China, he is a feminine goddess of mercy, called Kuan Yin, and in Japan, Kwannon.

avadana

Buddhist narrative telling the deeds of saintly souls.

avatara

Descent; in particular, the descent of a deity from heaven who is incarnated on earth, usually referring to the Hindu god Vishnu. His avataras have included his incarnation as a fish; a boar; a tortoise; a man-lion; a dwarf;

Rama with an axe; the gentle Rama, hero of
the Ramayana; Krishna; the Buddha; and the
white horse Kalki, who is to appear at the end
of the age of Kali.

Avatarana

The abode of the Rakshasas.

avidya

Having no wisdom; ignorance.

Ayodhya

"Not conquered." Rama's capital in the
Indian epic poem, the Ramayana. Also, a
contemporary city in North India.

Ayutthaya

A kingdom which flourished in Thailand
between 1350 and 1776. Art produced
during this period is
classified as Ayutthaya
style. Also, the name of
a contemporary city in
Thailand. The name is
derived from the Indian
"Ayodhya."

B

bai raka

An ornamental crest
running along the barge
boards on the gable
ends of a roof.

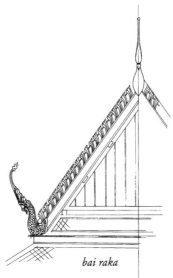

bai raka

bai sema

bai sema

Stone marker at the eight cardinal points around an ubosot delineating consecrated ground over which the ubosot is erected. Bai sema may be placed singly or in pairs; pairs sometimes indicate that the temple has undergone a major renovation or was built on the site of a former temple, at which time a second stone was added. Bai sema are often in the shape of a bodhi leaf and sheltered under a small square structure in a temple-like design.

bai sri

A conical arrangement of flowers or leaves used during auspicious ceremonies. Its appearance in a traditional Thai painting often indicates that a wedding is taking place.

Bakheng

Temple dedicated to Shiva built by King Yasovarman I at the beginning of the 10th century C.E. in Angkor.

Balarama

The older brother of Krishna and avatara of Vishnu.

baluster

A short post or pillar in a series that supports and forms a balustrade.

Banaspati

The combination of the kala and makara in East Java. See **Panaspati.**

Ban Chiang

The prehistoric civilization in Northeast Thailand with artifacts revealing a metal culture, dating from between 3600 and 2500 B.C.E., and extensive pottery production, including funerary vessels with distinctive lineal designs painted red-on-buff.

bangla

A curved-roof style found on brick temples, influenced by the thatched roofs in Bengal.

banteay

Citadel. A Khmer temple with an important enclosing wall.

baoli

A rectangular well surrounded by steps, found in Gujarat and West India.

Baphuon

An 11th-century C.E. Khmer temple in Angkor, Cambodia. Also refers to the 11th-century C.E. school of Khmer art.

baradari

Twelve-pillared. A portico or pavilion with columns, found in India.

Ban Chiang-style pottery

baray

A man-made reservoir or lake.

barge board

The frame of the two sloping edges of a gable-style roof. On Thai temples, the barge board is often in the form of a naga decorated with a bai raka, the head of the naga turned upward at the lower end of the board.

bas-relief

Sculpture in low relief, with the figures projecting only slightly from the background.

bat

A monk's alms bowl.

Bayon

Khmer temple built by King Jayavarman VII in the city of Angkor Thom. Also applies to the Khmer school of art from the late 12th to the early 13th centuries C.E.

B.E.

Buddhist Era. The Theravada tradition claims that the Buddha's parinirvana occurred in the year 544 B.C.E., marking the beginning of the Buddhist era in Burma, Sri Lanka, and India. In Thailand, Laos and Cambodia the era begins on the first anniversary of that event, in 543 B.C.E. Thus, for example, a Thai B.E. date may be converted to C.E. by subtracting 543.

belfry

A bell tower.

beki

A circular stone below the amalaka in the finial of a North Indian–style temple. See **amalaka** illustration.

bencharong

Five colors. A type of enameled porcelain composed of five colors against a sixth background color which was made in China according to Thai specifications, for export to Thailand. This porcelain first appeared in the late Ayutthaya period and continued until the reign of King Chulalongkorn (Rama V), when European ware replaced the bencharong in popularity. Later fewer colors were sometimes used but the origins and manufacture of the ware were similar and the name bencharong continued to apply.

bencharong

betel set

Containers and equipment, usually with a tray, used to hold and prepare the ingredients for betel chewing, a long-standing tradition in Southeast Asia. Ingredients include an areca-nut, betel leaf, and lime paste. The betel set can be made of precious metals, ceramic, wood, or woven fibers.

betel set

bhadra

The flat side of a shikhara or Indian temple tower.

Bhadrakali

Tantric goddess who is the consort of Bhairava.

bhadrapitha

A rectangular pedestal for a deity.

Bhagavad Gita

Hindu religious text prescribing a moral and ethical code of behavior emphasizing the merit of selfless service and devotion.

Bhairava

Shiva in his fearful aspect as a ten-armed being, wearing a necklace made of bones and a skull as a hair ornament.

bhakti

Devotion. A type of worship in which the devotee seeks union with his personal god through intense devotion in the hope of releasing his or her soul.

Bharata

Half-brother of Rama in the Indian epic poem, the Ramayana.

Bhattara-Guru

A form of Shiva popular in Java, recognized as a fat, bearded ascetic with plaited hair, sometimes holding a jar, rosary, or fly whisk. At one time worshiped in Java as the rishi Agastya.

bhavan

An Indian building or house.

bhikku

An ordained Buddhist monk; a religious mendicant.

bhikkuni

Feminine form of bhikku; a Buddhist nun. Although Theravada Buddhism originally provided for an order of nuns, it was discontinued centuries ago. The white-robed women with shaved heads seen in Thai monasteries are lay persons without official status who live according to Buddhist precepts. Also called mae chi in Thailand.

Bhima

Important character in the Indian epic, the Mahabarata, famous for his strength and bravery. The son of Vayu, the god of wind, he is of vast size and usually depicted carrying a club.

Bhimsena

See **Bhima**.

bhoga-mandapa

The refectory hall of Hindu temples found in Orissa.

bhumi

Earth. Refers to a horizontal molding running down the length of a shikhara, an Indian temple tower.

bhumisparsamudra

The hand gesture of the Buddha, "calling the earth to witness," also known as "victory

bhumisparsamudra

over Mara" and indicating the moment of enlightenment. In this mudra the right hand is resting on the right knee with fingers pointing downward while the left hand lies in the lap, palm facing upward. The Buddha makes this gesture while seated in a half-lotus position.

boar

An incarnation of the Hindu god Vishnu, known as Varaha.

Bodh Gaya

The place where the Buddha attained bodhi or enlightenment, located near the town of Gaya in Bihar state of North India.

bodhi

The perfect knowledge or enlightenment which enables one to become a buddha.

bodhimanda

The sacred spot at Bodh Gaya where the Buddha attained enlightenment.

bodhisattva

One whose essence is perfect knowledge. A being who has attained enlightenment (bodhi) but has postponed Buddhahood in order to help others. In Mahayana Buddhism, many bodhisattvas are personifications of divine qualities such as compassion (Avalokitesvara) or wisdom (Manjushri) and are often depicted with multiple arms. In both Theravada and Mahayana Buddhism, the term is also applied to the earlier lives of the historical Buddha and to his former life as a prince.

bodhi tree

The sacred fig tree in Bodh Gaya under which the Buddha attained bodhi or enlightenment. After the original tree was cut in 600 C.E., cuttings were replanted where ever Theravada Buddhism was introduced and practiced.

bodhi tree

bonze

A Buddhist monk in Burma.

Borobudur

Great Buddhist monument built in Java by the Sailendra kings between 778 and 824 C.E. A nine-tiered mountain-like structure, it rises to a height of 34.5 m. It is decorated with five kilometers of reliefs, ornamented with five hundred Buddha images, and constructed of more than one million andesite stones, or volcanic rock, mined from riverbeds. Symbolically Borobudur is at the same time a stupa, a replica of the cosmic mountain Mt. Meru, and a mandala.

bot

Ubosot. The ordination hall of a Thai

monastery which is on consecrated ground marked with bai sema stones at each of the eight cardinal points.

boun

A Lao festival.

Brahma

The god of creation in the Hindu pantheon of gods which includes Vishnu the preserver and Shiva the destroyer. Brahma is brought forth from the golden lotus which grows from the navel of Vishnu during his cosmic sleep in order to begin each new round of crea-

tion. He is usually depicted with four heads, and four arms which may carry any of the following attributes: disc, ladle, scepter, string of beads, bow, water jug, fly whisk, or the Vedas. His vehicle is the hamsa and his consort is Sarasvati, the goddess of learning. In Buddhist art especially during the Dvaravati period, he is frequently depicted with one head and two arms as an attendant of the Buddha along with Indra.

Brahma

Brahma heavens

In Buddhist mythology, the sixteen heavens of form without sensory perception that exist above the six lower heavens.

Brahman

The universal world spirit which is all pervading, absolute, and eternal in Hindu philosophy. It is the source of all creation, animate and inanimate. It is also the highest social category in the Hindu caste system, and the only caste from which a priest can come.

Brahmanism

An early form of Hinduism during the Vedic period in India. The religion was brought to India by the Aryans during the second millenium B.C.E.

Brahmanaspati

A composite animal combining features of the mounts of the three main Hindu gods: the beak of Vishnu's Garuda, the horns of Shiva's bull, and the wings of Brahma's hamsa. The Buddha mounted on such a creature represents the ascendancy of Buddhism over Hinduism.

Brihaspati

The lord of prayer, an Aryan deity in the Vedic period who was worshiped as a great sage and served as a model and teacher to other gods. Associated with the planet Jupiter.

Buddha

Awakened or Enlightened One. One who has achieved the highest knowledge of truth and is thereby freed from all further rebirth. The historical Buddha or Shakyamuni Buddha who was the founder of Buddhism. He was born as Prince Siddhartha in 563 B.C.E., attained enlightenment at the age of thirty-five, and died at the age of eighty, in approximately 483 B.C.E. The basis of his teachings are the Four Noble Truths and the Noble Eightfold Path. In Hinduism, Buddha is the ninth incarnation of Vishnu.

Buddhapada

Footprint of the Buddha.

Buddhism

Buddhism is the religion or body of thought based on the teachings of the historical Buddha, Siddhartha Gautama, emphasizing compassion for all sentient beings, non-attachment, and release from suffering through the attain-

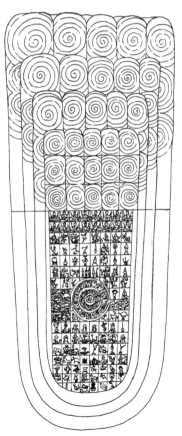

Buddhapada

ment of enlightenment. This can be achieved by following the guidelines of the Four Noble Truths and the Noble Eightfold Path. After the death of the Buddha two main schools of Buddhism evolved: Mahayana and Hinayana (Theravada).

Buddhist Lent

The three-month period during the rainy season when monks retreat to the monasteries to study and refrain from traveling.

bull

The vehicle of the Hindu god Shiva known as Nandi, the symbol of male strength, virility, and potency. It is also found represented in the pre-Aryan art of the Indus Valley civilization.

C

candi

A generic term used in Indonesia for all ancient temples, both Hindu and Buddhist.

capital

Uppermost part of a column, pillar, or pilaster, usually decorated.

celadon

Pottery ware with a blue-green to gray glaze, produced originally in China and later in other countries such as Thailand.

cella

Temple chamber housing the image or symbol of a god.

cetiya

See **chaitya**.

chaitya: two variations

chaitya

Sanctuary. An assembly hall for meditation and teaching. Originally an apsidal hall housing a stupa, or a funerary mound enshrining sacred relics of the Buddha, or objects used by him, or the relics of his disciples. Also refers to a particular style of arch and window in early cave temples in India.

chakra, Chakra

Wheel, disc, or symbol of the sun, attribute of the god Vishnu. Also, the Wheel of the Law, symbol of the doctrine which the Buddha set in motion when he gave his first sermon; symbol of the eternal cycle of birth, death, and rebirth; one of the marks of an enlightened being; a center of spiritual energy in the body.

chakravartin

"Universal monarch." Term applied to the Buddha, the spiritual ruler of the universe.

Chakri

The dynasty that has reigned in Thailand since 1782.

Cham

People inhabiting central and southern Vietnam since ancient times, probably of Indonesian origin. They founded an Indianized kingdom called Champa, and produced a unique style of architecture and sculpture, known as Cham art between the 7th and 17th centuries C.E.

Cham art

Champa

An early Indianized kingdom in the coastal areas of central and southern Vietnam, existing from the 2nd to the 15th centuries C.E. It was briefly controlled and annexed by Cambodia (1181–1220), then gradually absorbed by the Vietnamese from the late 10th to 17th centuries C.E. Important archaeological Cham sites are located in the Danang region of present-day Vietnam.

Chamunda

Goddess of death and destruction; one of the fierce aspects of Devi, the consort of the god Shiva.

chanak

An eagle, a Vajrayana Buddhist symbol.

Chandra

The moon god.

Channa

The male servant of Prince Siddhartha, the historical Buddha.

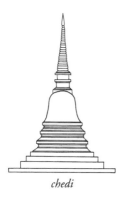

chedi

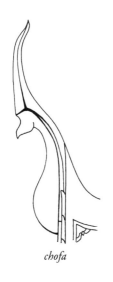

chofa

chao

A title denoting greatness, used in Thailand and Laos.

chattra

Umbrella or parasol held over an honored figure, as a symbol of royalty, domination, protection, honor. It also crowns the mast of a Buddhist stupa or chedi.

chedi

Chaitya or cetiya; a monument to enshrine the relics of the Buddha or his disciples, a reminder of the Buddha, or the ashes of the dead.

Chenla

The Chinese name for a state in Cambodia that existed between the 6th and 8th centuries C.E.

Chiang Saen

A town in northern Thailand. Also, the art style produced during the 12th and 13th centuries C.E. in northern Thailand.

Chintamani Lokesvara

"Lord of the universe with a wishing gem." A form of the bodhisattva Avalokitesvara.

Chintha

Burmese name for the stylized lion seen guarding temples.

chofa

A bunch of sky; sky-tassel. The finial on

either end of the roof peak of Buddhist temples in Thailand. Shaped like a stylized bird's head, it symbolizes either Garuda, the mount of the god Vishnu, or hamsa, the mount of the god Brahma.

Chola

A dynasty and kingdom in South India during the 10th to 13th centuries C.E. Also a style of art specially known for its bronze sculpture.

chorten

Tibetan word for stupa or chedi; miniature stupa.

chua

Vietnamese term for pagoda.

Chunda

A Vajrayana Buddhist goddess, one of the Taras.

colonette

Small decorated column positioned on either side of a doorway, often used in Khmer architecture.

conch shell

One of the emblems of the Hindu god Vishnu representing the primordial sound. Used in Hindu and Buddhist rituals.

corbelling

A technique of constructing an arch or roof using an overlapping arrangement of stones.

cornice

An ornamental molding along the top of a wall, pillar, or building.

D

dado

Part of a pedestal, between the base and cornice. Also the lower section of a wall.

dagoba

A relic, shrine, or stupa, in Sri Lanka.

dakini

Female divinity of low rank in Vajrayana Buddhism. There are two forms, malevolent and benevolent. There is a group of five dakinis associated with the five jinas, each holding a jewel, a lotus, or a double thunderbolt. A dakini may be distinguished from an apsara by the presence of a third eye in the middle of the forehead. In Hinduism, dakinis are female imps who wait upon Kali and feed on human flesh.

Daksha

Able, competent, intelligent. Usually associated with the idea of creative power. Daksha is the son of Brahma.

Dandadhara

"The rod-bearer." A name given to Yama, the god of death.

darbas

Rakshasas and other destructive demons.

dargah

A Muslim tomb complex or shrine.

Daruka

Krishna's charioteer and the companion who attended him in his final days.

darwaza

A door or gateway.

den

A temple of a deified hero in Vietnam.

dentil

A small block used as part of a cornice.

deva

A god of undetermined rank. There are said to be thirty-three in number, eleven for each of the three worlds of Buddhist cosmology.

Devadatta

A jealous cousin of the Buddha who plotted to harm him.

deval

A memorial pavilion built to mark a funeral pyre in India.

devaraja

King of the gods. A title often applied to Indra and the Buddha. In Java and Cambodia, a cult of devaraja developed which

devata

claimed that the king was an emanation of a god and would be reunited with that god after death.

devata
   A female deity in Cambodian art.

devi, Devi
   A goddess of undetermined rank. The shakti or consort of Shiva, and a goddess with many forms. Her mild forms are Uma (light), Sati (the virtuous one), Annapurna (the bestower of good deeds), Haimavati (born of the Himalayas), Jagamata (mother of the world), and Bhavani (the female creator). Her terrible forms are Durga (inaccessible), Kali (black), Shyama (black), Chandi (fierce), and Bhairavi (terrible).

deul
   The residence of a deity. The main shrine of a Hindu temple.

dhamma
   See **dharma**.

dhammapala
   See **dharmapala**.

dharma, Dharma
   Law, truth, reality, or righteousness. In Theravada Buddhism, it refers to the teachings of the Buddha as found in the Tripitaka.

dharmachakra

The Wheel of the Law, a symbol of the Buddha's first sermon. The wheel also symbolizes the setting in motion of the Buddha's philosophy. In sculpture, the wheel is often depicted with a pair of deer because the Buddha's first sermon was preached in the deer park at Sarnath in North India.

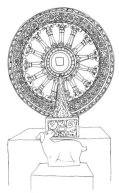

dharmachakra

dharmachakramudra

A hand gesture of a Buddha image setting in motion the Wheel of the Law, symbolizing the teaching of the Buddha. Both hands are held out at chest level. The right hand is palm out, the left hand palm in, with forefingers and thumbs forming two circles. The circles of the two hands either touch or interlock.

dharmapala

A guardian or defender (pala) of the Buddhist law (dharma). In Vajrayana Buddhism, the dharmapalas wage war against the demons and enemies of the faith. They have a terrifying appearance.

Dharmasastra

Ancient books of the law in Hinduism.

dharmachakramudra

dhoti

An Indian male garment consisting of a piece of cloth draped around the lower part of the body.

dhyana

An advanced stage of meditation.

dikka

A raised platform around an ablution tank.

dikpala

dikpala

Guardian of one of the four cardinal points, or the four directions of the sky, who protects the world from demons. Dikpalas are often depicted on Hindu temples facing in different directions. There are eight listed dikpalas who guard the four main and four intermediate directions.

dinh

The village communal house in Vietnam composed of two parallel wings. Often decorated with the dragon, unicorn, tortoise, and phoenix, the four animals associated with happiness. The dinh is where the guardian spirit of the village resides. It provides a place for private worship and public ceremonies.

dipdan
A lamp pillar found in Indian architecture.

diwan-i-am
A hall of public audience in Indian palaces.

do-chala
Rectangular Bengali-style roof.

dok-sofa
A frond-like ornament which surmounts temple roofs in Laos. It may be described as "a bucket of flowers." Ten or more flowers indicate the temple was built by a king.

Dona
A Brahmin sage who divided the relics of the Buddha among eight warring kings after the Buddha's cremation.

Dong Duong
Center of Cham art and culture which supplanted the city of My Son from the time King Indravarman II built a Buddhist monastery there at the end of the 9th century C.E. It remained the locus of Cham art and culture for less than a century.

Dongson
A village on the Ma River in Vietnam. The name applies to a culture that produced high-

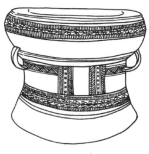

Dongson drum

quality bronze-work between 500 and 200 B.C.E., and also refers to the decorated bronze drums of various types and sizes produced and used for ritual purposes. The Dongson drums are considered the first and finest of Southeast Asian works of art.

dtin sin

A decorative border on a tubular skirt in Laos.

dukha

Suffering, unhappiness, misery. The first of the Four Noble Truths of Buddhism.

dukkha

See **dukha**.

durbar

The court of an Indian ruler or governor. Also a square surrounded by buildings.

Durga

A form of Devi, the consort of Shiva, who

rides a tiger or lion. She is frequently depicted in Indian and Javanese art as slaying the buffalo demon Mahishasura with weapons of the gods.

dvarapala

A guardian of a temple door or gate often holding a club or mace. In Southeast Asia, it guards the entrances to temples.

Durga

Dvaravati

The name of a kingdom in Thailand populated by the Mon people, existing between the 6th and 11th centuries C.E. The name also applies to the art produced during that period.

E

earth goddess

In Buddhism, the earth goddess Toranee is called before the demon Mara to bear witness to the merit the Buddha accumulated in his previous lives. In the iconography of Thailand and Cambodia the earth goddess wrings water from her long hair, still wet from the lustral libation made by the future Buddha in

eave bracket

the course of his previous lives, and the water from her hair drowns the armies of the demon Mara.

eave bracket

Architectural term used to describe the ornament supporting the roof eaves. On Buddhist temples in Thailand the eave bracket is often in the shape of a naga or mythical serpent, or a figure.

Eightfold Path

The Eightfold Path is the last of the Four Noble Truths of the Buddha's teaching. It outlines the eight steps one should follow in order to eliminate suffering and thus attain enlightenment or nirvana. The eight steps are: right understanding, right thought, right speech, right action, right livelihood, right effort, right mindfulness, and right concentration.

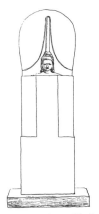

ekamukhalinga: two variations

ekamukhalinga

Representation of a linga with a single face.

elephant terrace

Terrace showing elephants in relief, built in front of the Royal Palace at Angkor Thom by King Jayavarman VII in the 12th century C.E.

Ellora

A total of thirty-four caves of religious significance, including Buddhist (600–800 C.E.), Hindu (600–900 C.E.) and Jain (800–1100 C.E.). The interiors are carved with religious sculptures, architectural ornamentation, and relief panels. This is a World Heritage site.

Emerald Buddha

A dark-green jasper Buddha image housed in the Emerald Buddha Temple in Bangkok, regarded as the guardian spirit or palladium of the kingdom of Thailand.

Erawan

The Thai name given to the three-headed elephant Airavata, produced during the churning of the ocean of milk. He is the symbol of the clouds and vehicle of the Hindu god Indra.

enlightenment

True understanding or perfect knowledge.

epigraph

A carved inscription.

F

fakir

A Muslim who has taken a vow of poverty.

farang

Thai word for a white-skinned foreigner,

derived from a word referring to France.

faience

A mixture of sand and clay which, when baked, fuses into a glass-like material. Often used for colored tile work.

fauwara

A fountain used for ritual ablutions in a mosque.

feng shui

Natural elements of wind and water used in a geomantic system which determines the orientation of dwellings, cities, and graves in order to harmonize correctly with nature. A dousing rod and astrological compass are used for this purpose.

festoon

Ornament resembling a garland of flowers or fruit.

Four encounters; Four passing sights

The four sights encountered by Prince Siddhartha which made him renounce his princely life and become an ascetic. In Theravada Buddhism, the four sights are an old man, a sick man, a dead man, and a wandering ascetic.

Four Noble Truths

The basic teachings of the Buddha. The First Noble Truth is that suffering exists; the second is that suffering is caused by clinging to that which is pleasant; the third is that after discovering the origin of suffering one can put an end to it; and the fourth is the Noble Eightfold Path, the way leading to the cessation of suffering.

filigree
Delicate ornamental work of metallic thread, usually made of gold or silver.

finial
An ornament placed on the top of a stupa, tower, dome, or other architectural feature. Also found on the covers of vessels.

foliation
Ornamental carved or painted leaf-like design.

fresco
Usually a mural painting done by applying mineral or earth pigments onto wet lime plaster.

frieze
Horizontal band of figures or decorative designs.

fronton
The French name for pediment.

Funan
According to Chinese chronicles, an Indianized state founded in the 1st century C.E., and the precursor to Cambodia. It dominated the Mekong and Chao Phya valley regions between the 2nd and 6th centuries C.E.

G

gable board

Gandhara-style sculpture

gable board

In Thai architecture, the recessed face of a pediment on the gable end of a building. It is triangular in shape, and is located between the two slanting roof eaves and the horizontal tie beam. Corresponds to the Western architectural term tympanum.

gada

A mace or club. One of Vishnu's attributes.

gandhabbas

See **gandharvas**.

gandharvas

Male celestial musicians, companions of the apsaras.

Gandhara style

The art style developed during the Kushan period of Indian history, from the 1st to 2nd centuries C.E. It is distinguished by the depiction of the Buddha with realistic features wearing draped robes reflecting Greek influence.

Ganesha

The elephant-headed son of Shiva and Parvati. He is the god of knowledge and intelligence, and the remover of obstacles. He is represented as an obese human figure with the head of an elephant. His mount is a rat.

Ganesha

Ganga

Goddess personifying the River Ganges, or Ganga, in India. Her symbol and vehicle is the makara. The River Ganges is considered a holy river by Hindus.

Garuda

A mythical divine bird, the vehicle of the Hindu god Vishnu. He is king of birds and enemy of the nagas or serpents. He is depicted with a human body, and the wings, legs, and beak of a bird. In Thailand, the Garuda is used as a royal symbol linking the Thai monarch to the powerful Vishnu.

Ganga

Gautama

The name given to the historical Buddha by his clan, the Shakyamuni.

geomancy

The Chinese art of divination by lines and figures used to determine the correct placement of objects and buildings.

Garuda

ghanta

A bell, sometimes held in the hand of a deity. Its sound is symbolic of existence. As an attribute of the Hindu god Shiva, it symbolizes creation. In Buddhism, it can represent wisdom.

ghat

An Indian architectural feature consisting of steps or a platform at the edge of a body of water, used as a place for bathing.

gokhala

A niche in a Jain temple.

gold leaf

Gold which has been hammered and made tissue-paper thin and then cut into one-inch squares. These are then applied to religious objects for decoration or to make merit.

Golden Temple

The Golden Temple at Amritsar in the Punjab. The foundation for the temple was laid during the period of the fifth guru, Arjan Dev (1581–1606). This temple is of the utmost importance to the Sikh community because it contains the holy book compiled by the fifth guru and more than five hundred hymns composed by five gurus and saints.

Gopa

The wife of Prince Siddhartha, also called Yashodhara.

gopis
Milkmaids, or female cowherds, who played with Krishna.

gopura
An ornamental crowned gateway or entrance to a religious sanctuary.

Gotama
See **Gautama**.

Govardhana
A mountain lifted by the Hindu god Krishna to shelter the herdsmen and their cattle from the storm caused by Indra.

Govinda
"Cowherd." One of the names of Krishna.

gopura

Great departure
The time when Prince Siddhartha, at the age of twenty-nine, left his family and princely life to become an ascetic in order to seek the cause of human suffering.

Great renunciation
Prince Siddhartha's silent and sad farewell to his wife, his baby son, and his royal heritage in order to become an ascetic.

Gupta-style sculpture

Gupta

A powerful dynasty located in the Ganges valley between 320 and 535 C.E. Also, the style of art that emerged in northern India during this period, considered to be the classic period of Indian art.

guru

Spiritual leader and teacher.

gurudwara

A Sikh religious complex, generally with a temple and a rest house.

H

Haj

The Muslim pilgrimage to Mecca. Every devout Muslim aspires to make the journey to Mecca at least once in his lifetime. This pilgrimage is known as the third pillar of Islam.

Hampi

Founded in the 14th century, this was a great Hindu center, and the seat of the Vijayanagara Empire for more than two hundred years. Today it is a vast ruins located on the right bank of the Tungbhadra River in South India.

hamsa

A sacred goose, gander, or swan. The vehicle of the god Brahma. In his flight, the hamsa establishes a link between the aquatic world and the heavens. Seen frequently in Buddhist imagery.

Hanuman

The son of the wind god Vayu. He was a semidivine monkey who assisted Rama in his struggle with Ravana in the Indian epic poem, the Ramayana.

hamsa

Harappan

The name given to a civilization which flourished in the Indus valley between 2300 and 1750 B.C.E., Harappa being one of its most important city settlements. Other important city sites are those of Mohenjodaro, and Kalibangan. The most important surviving artifacts include miniature stone sculptures, numerous terra-cotta figurines, seals, as well as bronze female figures.

Hanuman

harem

The women's quarters in a Muslim dwelling.

Hari-Hara

Hindu divinity who combines the names and features of Vishnu (Hari) and Shiva (Hara). The deity is a combination of these two gods. On one side of his head is Vishnu's crown, and on the other is Shiva's plaited locks; he holds the main attributes of both gods.

harmika

The railing surrounding the dome of an Indian stupa.

haveli

A mansion of more than one story built around an inner courtyard usually found in western India.

hera

A mythical monster often seen at the end of an arch in Thailand. Its teeth meet its nostrils, it has the body of a naga, and it often spews from its open mouth another creature, flowers, or a flame-like motif.

Hevajra

A protective god in Tantric Buddhism with the rank of a buddha. He has eight heads, sixteen arms, and two or four legs. He has a third eye. In Cambodia and Thailand he is seen in a dancing posture with his left leg crushing a demon and his right leg bent with

the foot touching the left leg above the knee.
He wears ornaments. In Tibet he is usually
depicted in yabyum with his consort.

Hijra

Muhammed's flight from Mecca to Medina
in 622 C.E., the year from which the Muslim
calendar is dated.

Himaphan

A mythical forest located in the Himalayas,
below the heavens of the gods. Often mentioned in Buddhist literature, it is inhabited
by both real and imaginary animals.

Himavat

See **Himaphan**.

Hinayana

"Lesser vehicle," a derogatory term applied
to one branch of Buddhism by Mahayana
Buddhists. The Hinayana school of
Buddhism is closest to the original teachings
of the Buddha. At one time there were many
sects of Hinayana Buddhism; today only
Theravada remains. It is practiced in Sri
Lanka and mainland Southeast Asia.

Hinduism

The main religious and social system in
India, of ancient origin. Hindus share a
common belief in the law of karma, the
transmigration of the soul, and a universal
spirit or Brahman. Hindu religious practices
include the worship of several gods and
goddesses.

hintha

A mythical bird in Burma.

Hoa-lai

The art style of Champa in Vietnam in the first half of the 9th century C.E.

Holi

Spring festival associated with the Hindu god Krishna.

ho klong

The drum tower in a Thai monastery.

ho rakhang

The bell tower in a Thai monastery.

ho trai

The library in a Thai monastery, usually built on stilts in a pond to prevent insects from destroying the manuscripts.

howdah

A seat on an elephant's back. It is usually made of wood, or sometimes ivory, and may be canopied.

hti

A decorative element in the shape of a lacy umbrella which often crowns the mast of a Buddhist stupa in Burma.

Hue

Political capital of Vietnam from 1802 to 1945 C.E. One of Vietnam's cultural, religious, and educational centers.

huzra

A chamber in a Muslim tomb.

hypostyle hall

A term used for a columned hall. Often the outermost and grandest part of a temple complex.

I

icon

An image, symbol, or picture of a sacred or religious subject or object. Principle votive image in a temple.

iconography

Illustration of a subject by means of drawings or figures. In religious art each deity has his or her own iconography, therefore the drawing must include particular details of anatomy, dress, posture, hand position, and attributes. A knowledgeable observer is able to recognize the deity by the presence of such features.

Id

Principal Muslim festival.

idgah

Open area for prayers during Muslim festivals, usually located to the west of a town.

ikat

A tie-dying method of making patterned fabrics.

imam

Muslim religious leader attached to a mosque.

Inao

A legend and classical dance drama introduced to Thailand from Java around 1760 C.E., near the end of the Ayutthaya period.

incarnation

The representation of a deity or spirit of a god in another form.

Indra

Vedic god of the heavens, weather, and war, wielding a thunderbolt. He is the king of the gods and the ruler of Tavatimsa heaven, a place on the summit of the mythical Mt. Meru. He also figures in Buddhism and is frequently found in legends of the life of the Buddha, often depicted along with Brahma as an attendant of the Buddha. He has a green complexion and may carry a thunderbolt, disc, elephant goad, or axe. His mount is the elephant Airavata or Erawan. In recent times his status has become less important than Vishnu and Shiva. He is the lokapala of the east in Hindu cosmology.

Indrani

Consort of the Hindu god Indra.

Indus valley

See **Harappan**.

iryapatha

Four positions of the body—walking, standing, sitting, and reclining—in which the Buddha may be represented.

Ishana

A guardian of the northeast. Also a name of Shiva or Rudra.

Ishvara

Lord. A title given to the Hindu god Shiva.

Islam

The Muslim religion based on a belief in one supreme God and on the teachings of Muhammad, his prophet. The five precepts of Islam are: the profession of faith, prayer, pilgrimage, fasting, and charity. These may be symbolized by an open hand.

J

jaba

The front court of a Balinese temple.

jaba tengah

The central court of a Balinese temple.

jadu

Magic.

jaga mohan

Audience hall or antechamber in front of the sanctuary in an Orissan temple in India.

Jagadambi

"Mother of the world." Parvati.

Jagannath

"Lord of the world." Particularly Krishna, worshiped at Puri in Orissa, India.

jagati

A railed parapet, a feature in Indian architecture.

Jahnu

A sage who, during his devotions, was once disturbed by the noise of the Ganges River, so he drank up its waters. He later relented, allowing the stream to flow out from his ear. Hence, the Ganges (Ganga) is called Jahnavi, daughter of Jahnu.

Jainism

The Jain religion was founded in North India by a revered ascetic named Vardhamana, who became known as Mahavir, "great hero." The Jains base their entire system of values and ethics on ahimsa, a doctrine often translated as the non-harming of all living things. Like Hinduism, Jainism maintains a belief in karma. Like Buddhism, Jainism began as a reform movement of the Brahmanic religious beliefs of the 6th century B.C.E. but never spread beyond India. The two main sects are Digambara and Svetambara.

jali

A lattice or perforated pattern on a screen or window opening, seen in India.

Jambhala

The god of wealth in Mahayana Buddhism. Counterpart of Kuvera, the god of wealth in Hinduism.

Jambupati

A mythical Indian emperor who was too vain to listen to the Buddha's teachings. The Buddha changed himself into a great and magnificent emperor and invited Jambupati to visit him. The experience changed Jambupati and made him receptive to the Buddha's teachings. This story is a Southeast Asian addition to the legend of the Buddha and does not appear in the Buddhist literature of India or Sri Lanka.

jami masjid

A congregational mosque.

Jamuna

A river in North India, also personified as a Hindu goddess who rides a tortoise.

Janaka

Father of Sita in the Indian epic poem, the Ramayana.

jangha

A broad band of sculpture situated in the middle of an exterior temple wall.

Jara

"Old age." The hunter who unwittingly killed Krishna.

jata

Braided and matted chignon of hair worn by Shiva, rishis, and ascetics.

Jataka

The 547 stories of the previous lives of the Buddha in the course of his long progression to his final birth. Three extra lives were added in Burma for reasons of symmetry in mural painting. The last ten stories before his final birth as Prince Siddhartha are the most popular and the most important.

jatamukuta

The matted and coiled hair of Shiva as an ascetic. Often depicted as an elaborate headdress.

jawab

A building which duplicates another building to provide symmetry in Indian architecture.

jaya stambha

A victory tower.

jhilmil

A projecting canopy over a window or doorway, a feature of Indian architecture.

jina

Conqueror or victorious one. In Jainism,

a tirthanka. In Buddhism, the term designates the historical Buddha or the five transcendental buddhas of the Mahayana sect. Each jina buddha is assigned to a specific location in Buddhist cosmology and is positioned accordingly on a mandala.

Jyotirlinga

The luminous energy of Shiva manifested miraculously in twelve holy places in India.

K

Kailasa

A mountain in the Himalayas. The dwelling place of Shiva and Parvati.

kala

Term used to express time and energy, death and creation, and the destruction of the universe. Personified as Mahakala, a form of Shiva, and as Kali or Mahakali, a form of his consort Devi. Both represent the terrifying destructive aspects of time.

kalachakra

A dance of time and eternity performed by Shiva.

kalamkari

Pen work, the term used for drawing and painting on cloth in the style of Andhra Pradesh in India.

kalan

kalan

A sanctuary tower in Cham religious architecture.

kalasa

A water pot believed to hold the amrita or water of life. Frequently one of the attributes of Padmapani, Kwan Yin, Maitreya, and Kuvera. In Hindu and Buddhist architecture the term is also used for the pinnacle crowning a stupa.

Kali

In Vedic times, this name meant "the black" and was associated with Agni, the god of fire, who had seven tongues with which to lick the offerings of butter. Of these seven, Kali was the black terrifying tongue. Now Kali refers to the terrifying manifestation of Devi, the consort of Shiva. She has a hideous, tusked face which is smeared with blood, and four arms, one of which holds a weapon and another, the head of a giant dripping with blood. Her other two arms are raised to bless worshipers. Her ornaments include snakes, skulls, and figures of children.

Kaliya

Serpent king with five heads subdued by Krishna.

Kali yuga

The present time cycle, the most depraved of the four cycles of present creations. It commenced in 3,102 B.C.E. and, according to

Brahmanic beliefs, will last four hundred and thirty-two thousand years.

Kalkin

The tenth avatara of Vishnu in the form of a white horse who will appear in the future. Riding the horse, Vishnu will carry a blazing sword enabling him to destroy evil and restore purity to the world.

kalpa

A day and night of Brahma, equal to 4,320 million years of mortals. The duration of a cosmic period.

kalayanamandapa

A hall with columns used for the symbolic marriage of the temple deity.

kama

Love or desire. In Hinduism, this has been personified as Kama, the god of love and desire, portrayed as the most handsome of all the gods. He carries a bow and arrows. In Buddhism, kama refers to objects of the senses as well as visible phenomena.

Kambuja

The ancient Khmers, supposedly descendants of Kambu Svayambhuva, their eponymous ancestor. The name is still in use in Cambodia.

kampheang kaew

Jeweled wall. A decorated wall built in a

temple or palace compound to separate a specially sacred area.

Kansa

Wicked king and uncle of Krishna, in Indian mythology.

Kanthaka

The horse owned by Prince Siddhartha, born on the same day as his master. After carrying the prince away from the palace on his "great departure," the horse died of a broken heart.

Kapilavatthu

The birthplace of the Buddha in ancient India, now in southern Nepal.

karawak

A mythical creature who combines the features of a human and a bird.

karma

The law of cause and effect. One's present life is the result of past actions, either in this life or in former lives. Karma ceases when one attains nirvana, and the cycle of births and deaths is broken. Karma is closely linked with samsara, or transmigration.

Karttikeya

The god of war, leader of Shiva's troops, usually considered to be the son of Shiva and Parvati. He is often depicted with six heads and six arms, carrying a double thunderbolt,

a sword, and a trident, and riding a peacock.
In Champa art, his mount is a rhinoceros. In
South India, he is known as Subrahmanya.
As the son of Shiva, he is called Kumara,
meaning prince, and is also known as Skanda.

Kassapa
A Buddha of the past; a predecessor of the
historical Buddha.

Kathin
A one-month period following the rainy
season or phansa, when lay people present
gifts and robes to Buddhist monks.

Kauravas
Descendants of Kuru, one branch of a royal
family figuring in the Indian epic, the Mahabharata.

kendi
A drinking vessel usually having a bulbous
spout and globular body.

kendi

Ketumati
The earthly paradise that Maitreya will
preside over when he descends as the Buddha.

Khmer
The ancient and modern inhabitants of
Cambodia. From the 7th to the 14th
centuries C.E., the Khmer established
a powerful kingdom based at Angkor from
which they ruled over much of Indochina.

khon mask

khon

A form of classical Thai theater, performed by masked dancers with a chorus and orchestra. The themes are taken from the Ramakien, the Thai version of the Indian epic poem, the Ramayana.

kinnara

Originally a mythical being who had a human body and the head of a horse, or vice versa. In later times it became a combination of a bird and a man or woman, with a human chest and head, and the wings and feet of a bird. In India, the kinnaras were a subgroup of heavenly musicians, or gandharvas.

kinnari

The female form of kinnara.

kirtimukha

The "face of glory" is usually represented as a face with two horns, round bulbous eyes, a human or lion's nose, a wide mouth with teeth, with or without a lower jaw. This term is used in India for the mask-like creature appearing above temple doorways. It is intended to drive away evil and protect the devout, in both Hindu and Buddhist mythology. The same creature is called kala in Cambodia, Indonesia, and Thailand.

kirtimukha

ko

A term used for bullock in Cambodia.

Koran

Sacred scriptures of Islam, a collection of Muhammad's oral revelations, said to be the words of Allah or God.

kranok

A flame-like design commonly used in Thailand.

kraton

Fortified villages in strategic positions from which local princes ruled ancient Indonesia.

kris

A short sword with a straight or curved blade, forged from iron ore and meteorite. It occupies an important place in Indonesian and Malaysian warfare. The handle of a ceremonial kris is highly decorated.

kranok

Krishna

"The dark one." The eighth and most popular incarnation or avatara of Vishnu. He is first mentioned in the Mahabharata where he delivers the Bhagavad Gita, "The Song of the Divine One," a religious poem of great significance, in which he reveals himself to be a supreme being. He is the most celebrated hero of Indian mythology.

krodha

Anger. A characteristic of certain Buddhist and Hindu deities. Their anger is meant to ward off enemies and protect the devout.

kru

A cavity inside a stupa filled with relics of Buddha images or precious objects presented to the Buddha.

Kshatriya

The warrior or ruling class in India, the second in the hierarchy of India's four traditional classes.

Kubera

See **Kuvera**.

Kulika

One of eight serpent kings who has a half moon on his head.

Kumara

A name of Skanda, the god of war.

Kumari

"The maiden." A name of Parvati before she became Shiva's consort.

kundala

An earring.

Kunti

Mother of the Kauravas and an important character in the epic poem, the Mahabharata.

Kurma

"Tortoise." Refers to the second avatara or descent of the Hindu god Vishnu.

Kuru

A prince of the Lunar race. He ruled in the northwest of India over the region near Delhi. His descendants were the Kauravas in the epic poem, the Mahabharata.

Kusa

One of Sita's twin sons, neither of whom were recognized by their father Rama until they were fifteen years old. The story appears in the Indian epic poem, the Ramayana.

Kusinagara

The place in North India where the Buddha died and where his remains were cremated and divided among eight kings. Originally known as Kushinara, it is one of the four major Buddhist pilgrimage sites.

kuti

Living quarters of a Buddhist monk in a Thai monastery.

Kuvalayapida

Demon in elephant form sent by Kansa to kill his nephew Krishna.

Kwan Yin

Kuvera

The god of wealth in Hinduism and Mahayana Buddhism. Often represented as an obese figure carrying a purse and accompanied by seven treasures. A god of the north, he rules over the yakshas and kinnaras.

Kwan Yin

The bodhisattva of compassion in Mahayana Buddhism in China, often represented as a female. See **Avalokitesvara.**

kyaung

A monastery or school in Burma.

L

lacquer

In Southeast Asia, an oleo-resin substance made from the puncturing of certain trees by a small insect. The secretion from the body of the insect combines with the sap of the tree and produces lacquer. It is a very durable substance which is waterproof and insect proof. It is used as a paint, inlay, and medium for incision or carving. Lacquer is used most often with gold leaf in architectural decoration or to decorate chests and bookcases used for religious texts.

lakhon

A traditional form of classical music in Thailand.

lakshana

A mark or auspicious characteristic of a great man. Especially applied to the thirty-two major marks described in Buddhist texts, whereby the predestination of the Buddha may be recognized at birth.

Lakshmana

A brother of Rama in the epic Indian poem, the Ramayana who shared Rama's exile and assisted him in the battle against Ravana.

Lakshmi

A consort of Vishnu. The goddess of beauty and good fortune. She was reincarnated with Vishnu as one of his avataras each time he appeared on earth. For example, she was born Sita, the wife of Rama, and Rukmuni the principal wife of Krishna. The lotus flower is one of her attributes.

Lakulisha

Founder of the Pashupati sect and believed to be an incarnation of the Hindu god Shiva. Usually depicted in art naked with an erect phallus.

Lalitavistara

A Sanskrit text which relates the traditional legend of the life of the Buddha.

lalitasana

A seated position with the left leg folded and the right leg hanging down.

Lamaism

A form of Buddhism practiced in Tibet and Mongolia.

Lanka

The city kingdom of Ravana, described in the Indian epic poem, the Ramayana, as huge and of great magnificence, with seven broad moats and seven stupendous walls of stone and metal. It is said to have been built of gold for the residence of Kuvera, from whom it was taken by Ravana.

Lan Na

A kingdom of North Thailand, centered in Chiang Mai, which flourished between the 13th and 14th centuries C.E.

laterite

A deposit of red or brown clay produced by decomposing rocks. Laterite is soft when first unearthed but becomes hard when exposed to the air. It is frequently used as a building material in Thailand and Cambodia.

Le

The dynasty ruling Vietnam from 1427 to 1789 C.E., the golden age of Vietnamese history when art flourished.

library

The name given to two separate buildings located on either side of the main entrance to a Khmer temple. There is no evidence they were used as libraries.

lime container

A container for holding lime paste used in betel chewing, made of metal or ceramic.

linga

A phallic emblem or representation of a male phallus, symbol of Shiva and his role in creation. It is called a mukhalinga when a face is added to its surface. There are many different types, often divided into three parts: a cubic base representing Brahma, an octagonal prism representing Vishnu, and a cylindrical section with a rounded top representing Shiva.

lingaparvata

A hill or mountain peak in the form of a linga.

lingum

See **linga**.

lintel

A crossbeam resting on two upright posts, usually decorated with narrative scenes or decorative motifs. In Khmer temples the lintel is above the door or window opening, directly below the pediment.

loka

World. A division of the universe. In general, the triloka or three worlds are heaven, earth, and hell. Another classification names seven worlds.

lokapala

World protector. In Hindu mythology there are eight lokapalas presiding over the eight directions. They are Indra (east); Agni (southeast); Yama (south); Surya or Nirriti (southwest); Varuna (west); Vayu (northwest); Kuvera (north); and Soma, Prithivi, or Shiva (northeast). In Buddhism there may be four, eight, ten, or fourteen lokapalas.

Lokesvara

"Lord of the world." He is a form of the bodhisattva Avalokitesvara, who was the center of a popular cult in ancient Cambodia. He is represented by the great faces on the towers of the Bayon temple and appears frequently in Khmer bas-reliefs.

Lopburi

A city in central Thailand which existed as early as the Dvaravati period, from the 6th to 11th centuries C.E., and served as a provincial capital under Khmer rule from the 11th to 14th centuries C.E. The name Lopburi also applies to the art produced in central Thailand during the Khmer period.

lost wax

A technique used in bronze casting. The technique of the Indianized Southeast Asian countries differs from that of China and the West.

lotus

A type of water lily associated with the divine birth story of the Buddha and used symbolically in Hindu and Buddhist art. According to the story, immediately after his birth the Buddha took seven steps, and wherever his feet touched the ground lotus flowers bloomed. Lotus pedestals are used as a base for some Buddha images.

lotus pedestals

luk nimit

A large round stone buried in the ground which serves as a boundary marker for the consecrated area used for the ubosot in a Thai monastery. Nine of these stones are used, one beneath the center of the ubosot, one at each corner and one at the center of each side. The positions of the last eight stones are marked above ground by bai sema stones.

Lumbini

The park near Kapilavatthu where Prince Siddhartha, the historical Buddha, was born. Located in present day Nepal.

luopon

The compass used by a geomancer to determine the auspicious orientation of buildings and tombs.

Maha-Bali

A king who became so powerful that he dominated the three worlds. Vishnu, in his dwarf incarnation, subdued him.

Mahabalipuram

A Hindu site of rock-cut temples and shrines in southern India built during the Pallava era dated to the mid 7th century C.E.

Mahabharata

Great epic poem from around the 5th century B.C.E. containing legends of Vedic times. It is composed of eighteen books consisting of two hundred and twenty thousand lines which chronicle the battle between the Kauravas and the Pandavas, two branches of a royal family. The Hindu god Krishna figures prominently in the epic.

mahadhatu

See **Mahathat**.

mahakala

See **kala** and **Kali**.

Maha Kassapa

The monk who succeeded the Buddha as the leader of the Sangha; usually depicted in murals as an old man along with the young monk Ananda, the Buddha's cousin and chief disciple.

mahal

A palace or grand building in India.

mahamandapa

A large enclosed hall in front of a main shrine.

Maha Maya

"Great illusion." Wife of King Suddhodana and mother of Prince Siddhartha who later became the Buddha. A male protective deity in Vajrayana Buddhism.

Mahaparinirvana

The great total extinction of the Buddha which took place at Kushinagara after he had gathered all his disciples to hear his final sermon in 483 B.C.E.

Maha Prajapati

The sister of Prince Siddhartha's mother, Maha Maya, who served as Siddhartha's guardian when his mother died seven days after his birth. She subsequently married his father, Suddhodana. Sometimes known as Gautami.

mahapurusha

A great man destined to become a world leader or savior, identified by the thirty-two lakshanas which are the markings of a future great being.

maharaja

Great king.

maharani

Great queen.

maharishi

Great teacher, rishi, or sage.

mahat

Great intellect produced at the creation.

Mahathat

Great relic; the name given to the most important reliquary monuments in Thailand.

mahatma

Great soul.

Mahavairochana

"Adi-Buddha; Great illumination or sun." One of the five jinas or transcendental buddhas of Vajrayana Buddhism. His position is in the center of a mandala making the gesture of supreme wisdom: the right index finger held in the left fist with the left thumb pointing upward. His symbols are the wheel and the sun.

Mahavamsa

The Pali chronicle tracing the history of Buddhism in Sri Lanka from its beginning in the 3rd century B.C.E. to the early 4th century C.E.

Mahavira

"Great hero." Last of the twenty-four tirthankaras or great teachers and the founder of the Jain religion. A contemporary of the Buddha.

Mahayana

"Greater vehicle." The "Great Way" branch of Buddhism which emphasizes reliance on bodhisattvas for those seeking salvation and liberation from the endless cycles of rebirth in their efforts to attain Buddhahood. This sect of Buddhism spread from northern India in the 2nd century C.E. and is practiced in countries of northern Asia, i.e. Nepal, China, Mongolia, Korea, Japan, Tibet, and Vietnam. At one time it was also practiced in Burma, Thailand, Cambodia, Malaysia, and Indonesia.

Maha-yogi

"The great ascetic." A name of Shiva.

Mahendraparvata

One of the seven chains of mountains of the Himalayas. The early name for Phnom Kulen in Cambodia.

Mahesvara

"The great lord." Shiva.

Mahishasuramardini

"Slayer of the buffalo demon." Durga's name when she is fighting Mahishasura, the buffalo demon who represents the forces of darkness and evil.

Mahishasura

The buffalo demon of darkness and evil who is slayed by Durga; in the Mahabharata, slayed by Skanda.

mahout

The driver and caretaker of an elephant.

Maitreya

A bodhisattva now residing in Tushita heaven who will be reborn as the future Buddha in order to renew the faith. He is revered in both the Theravada and Mahayana sects of Buddhism. He is sometimes portrayed as a bodhisattva ruling from his throne in heaven dressed in princely regalia. He wears a stupa in his headdress and often carries a vase and a wheel.

maithuna couples

Amorous couples often seen in erotic poses in Indian sculpture.

makara

A mythical sea creature representing abundance, used in architectural decoration, for example in combination with kala on doorway frames, lintels, or as balustrades. Sometimes depicted spouting another creature or plant from its mouth. In India, it has the body and tail of a fish, but in Southeast Asia, it has the body of a reptile. In Java, the head is similar to a crocodile's, with a large jaw and snout elongated into a trunk. In Champa, it has the head of a lion, with fangs and trunk, or the head of an antelope, with forelegs.

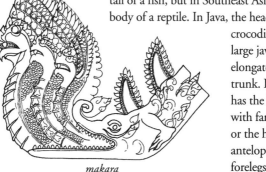

makara

manastambha

A free-standing pillar in front of a temple in India; also called a deepastambha.

mandala

A mystic diagram symbolizing the universe, used as an object of meditation in Vajrayana Buddhism. It usually contains an enclosing circle divided geometrically with representations of divinities or buddhas and their pantheons.

mandala

mandapa

In India, an open hall in front of the entrance to the sanctuary in a Jain or Hindu temple. In Thailand, an open-sided square-shaped building with a pyramidal roof used to shelter revered religious objects such as the footprint of the Buddha or the holy scriptures. In Khmer temples, the projecting porch entrance to the main shrine.

Mandara

The great mountain which the gods used for the churning of the ocean.

mandir

Temple.

mani

Gem. A mani wall is composed of stones with holy inscriptions at Buddhist sites.

Manibhadra

Guardian of travelers and chief of the yakshas.

Manjushri

Bodhisattva in Mahayana Buddhism who is the god of learning and wisdom. His symbol is a book and his vehicle is a lion.

Manmatha

A name of Kama, the god of love.

mantra

An incantation or verbal chant. A phonetic symbol which evokes and vivifies the divinity being worshiped. The sound of the mantra is more important than its meaning.

Mantrayana

See **Vajrayana**.

maqbara

Chamber of a Muslim tomb.

maqsura

Screen or arched façade of a mosque.

Mara

The demon god of sensual desires known as the tempter, who tries to prevent Gautama from attaining enlightenment and becoming the Buddha.

Maravijaya

"Victory over Mara." The epithet of the Buddha after he overcame the temptations of Mara and achieved enlightenment, symbolized by the bhumisparsamudra, the gesture of "calling the earth to witness."

maravijayamudra

See **bhumisparsamudra**.

Maruts

The storm gods, very prominent in the Vedas, represented as friends and allies of Indra.

masjid

A place of prostration; mosque.

math

Hindu or Jain monastery.

Mathura

One of the most sacred cities in Hinduism dating back to 600 B.C.E. located on the west bank of the Yamuna River. In the 7th century C.E. it was an important Buddhist center. The city was sacked and the Buddhist temples destroyed in 1017 C.E. Also a style of art.

matmi

A textile term of Laos and Thailand. A resist patterning process of tying off small bundles of yarn to prevent penetration of the dye, creating a pattern used in weaving. Also known as ikat.

Matris

Mothers; the divine mothers. Originally they appear to have been the female energies of the great gods. They are connected with Tantra worship and are represented worshiping Shiva.

Matsya

"Fish." Refers to Vishnu's first major avatara in the form of a fish.

Maurya

The dynasty founded by the Chandragupta at Patna, India, from 324 to 187 B.C.E. Also an art style.

mausoleum

A tomb.

maya

Illusion. Personified as a female created for the purpose of beguiling an individual.

mayura

Peacock. The vehicle of Skanda.

medallion

Circle or part of a circle framing a figure or decorative motif.

Meru

Mythical and sacred mountain at the center of the universe in Hindu and Buddhist cosmologies, with Tavatimsa heaven, abode of the god, Indra, and the thirty-three gods, at its summit. Multistoried religious buildings are often representations of Mt. Meru.

Metteya

See **Maitreya**.

middle way

In Buddhism, a path of no extremes; an acceptance of things as they are.

mihrab

Niche or arched recess in the western wall of a mosque to which worshipers turn for prayer.

mogul

European name for Indian emperors of the Mughal dynasty. See **Mughal**.

moksha

Union with the divine. In both Hinduism and Buddhism, it means the liberation from karma and the cycle of birth and death, and freedom from the cycle of time.

Mon

An ethnic group found in southern Burma; part of the Dvaravati kingdom existing in central Thailand from the 7th to 11th centuries C.E.

mondap

See **mandapa**.

Montagnard

Hill people; French reference to the hill tribes of Indochina.

moonstone

Semicircular decorated stone placed at the foot of steps or entrances to important buildings. Often decorated with animals, flowers, and birds.

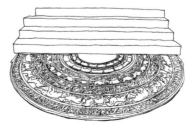

moonstone

mosque
A muslim house of worship.

Mrigadava
The deer park at Sarnath where the Buddha preached his first sermon setting in motion the Wheel of the Law.

Muchalinda
The naga king who protected the meditating Buddha from rain during the sixth week after his enlightenment by surrounding him with his coiled body and sheltering him with his multiheaded hood.

mudra
A symbolic gesture of the hands in Buddhist iconography; a mark or seal.

mudra: six variations

Mughal
Islamic dynasty founded in North India by Babur, who came to India from Central Asia. The dynasty ruled from 1526 C.E. until its final overthrow by the British. The Mughal rulers were great patrons of the arts.

Muhammad
Founder and prophet of the Islamic faith, born in Mecca in western Arabia in about 571 C.E. He died on 8 June 632 C.E.

mukhalinga
See **linga**.

mukuta

Tiara, diadem. Refers to a patterned head-dress fitting over the top of the head in Southeast Asian art.

My Son

The Hindu holy city in Da Nang province, Vietnam, built between the 7th and 13th centuries by the kings of Champa.

N

nak

See **naga**.

naga

A mythical serpent with the characteristics of a cobra, usually depicted as multiheaded or sometimes in human form. It serves as protector of the Buddha in meditation and as guardian of the earth's waters. It symbolizes fertility and abundance and is believed to be the progenitor of the Khmer race. Its struggles against Garuda are a common iconographic theme.

naga makara

Combination of naga and makara.

nagara

A city or capital. In India there are seven sacred cities which confer eternal happiness: Ayodhya, Mathura, Gaya, Varanasi, Kanchi, Avantika, and Dvaravati.

naga protecting the Buddha

nagaraja

King of the naga.

nakkar khana

A drum house; arched structure or gateway for musicians.

nal

Staircase in Indian architecture.

Nalagiri

The elephant that Buddha pacified when it was let loose to attack him by his jealous cousin, Devadatta.

nal mandapa

Porch over a staircase.

nandi mandapa

Portico or pavilion erected to shelter Nandi.

Nandi

The bull serving as Shiva's mount and symbol of fertility, found facing the main sanctuary in Shaivite temples. In paintings, usually depicted as white.

Nandikesvara

"Lord of Nandi." A form of Shiva popular in Java whose attributes are a lotus bud, jar, and trident. Guardian of doors, sometimes accompanied by Nandi.

Nandin

See **Nandi**.

nang thalung
Shadow puppet theater in Thailand.

Narasimha
"Man-lion." The fourth avatara of Vishnu with a man's body and lion's head.

Narasingha
See **Narasimha**.

Narayana
Another name for the Hindu god Vishnu.

nat
A Burmese spirit or god. There are thirty-seven in total, including local spirits, Hindu gods, and famous people who have died.

nat

nata mandapa
Dancing hall in a temple; usually the middle structure in an Orissan temple.

Nataraja
Shiva as "lord of the dance," representing cosmic truth or energy. His cosmic dance symbolizes creation, preservation, and destruction according to the divine order. He stands over a dwarf who represents ignorance.

Nataraja

navagraha
The nine planets, usually represented on a lintel or part of the decoration of the front door of a Hindu temple.

navaranga
The central hall of a temple.

ngyak

Mermaids who appear in Southeast Asian legends.

nibbhana

See **nirvana.**

niche

A recessed part of a wall usually containing a sculpture and framed by a pair of pilasters.

nielloware

Objects made from precious metals, usually silver or gold, and decorated with niello, a black composition consisting of metallic alloys of lead, copper, and silver which is fused with the metal object by heating. The process includes incising, heating, and polishing.

Nirriti

See **Surya.**

nirvana

The extinction or release from all suffering, desire, delusion, and future rebirths. The Buddhist state of enlightenment achieved while still on earth. Buddha reached nirvana under a bodhi tree.

niwas

A small palace or place of residence in India.

nyak

A mythical water serpent. See **naga.**

Nyi Loro Kidul
Goddess of the South Seas.

O

obelisk
A tapering four-sided shaft of stone with a pyramidal apex.

Oc Eo
The Neolithic culture originating in the Mekong delta province of An Giang in Vietnam around 100 C.E., which was a blend of Indian and indigenous culture. Some of the artifacts excavated reveal an ancient commercial port and cultural center which produced precious metals, multicolored stones, pottery, cauldrons, and monuments.

Odalan
A Balinese festival celebrating the anniversary of a temple.

ogee
A form of molding or arch with a double curved line comprising concave and convex parts, as in a chaitya. See **chaitya** illustration.

om
The most sacred mantra of the Hindus. Also written as aum.

oriel
A projecting window.

P

padma

The lotus flower, symbol of purity, creativity, and fertility; a universal symbol of Indian culture. Also serves as a pedestal upon which divine beings stand or sit.

Padma

Another name for the Hindu goddess Lakshmi in her role as earth mother.

Padmapani

"Lotus in hand." The bodhisattva Avalokitesvara in his role of creator, depicted with many small figures emanating from his body representing all the beings, divinities, and buddhas he has the power to create.

padmasana

A lotus throne, or the seated position of a deity with crossed legs forming a circular space like an open lotus.

Pagan

Burma's capital for 230 years, between the 11th and 13th centuries C.E., and city of Burma's golden age. Possibly founded in 849 C.E., its earliest structure dates from the late 9th century. The city was abandoned following the invasion of Kublai Khan in 1287. Over 2,217 pagodas are still standing among the remains of another 2,000 ruined temples. Also an art style.

pagoda

A sacred tower of several stories found in Burma, China, Korea, and Japan similar to a stupa or chedi. A Mahayana Buddhist temple, in Vietnam.

palanquin

A covered litter or chair seating one person and carried on poles.

Pala

The dynasty ruling Bihar and Bengal regions of northern India between the 8th and 12th centuries C.E. Also an art style.

Pali

A language of ancient India derived from Vedic Sanskrit and used by Theravada Buddhists in their sacred texts.

Pallava

A Hindu dynasty of southeast India which flourished between the 4th and 8th centuries C.E., and usually classified as the post-Gupta period (6th–8th century C.E.). An important period in art history.

Panaspati

"Lord of the jungle," in Thailand. Shiva in this form offers protection against the dangers and demons of the forest.

parinirvana

In Buddhism, the final nirvana following death, after which there will be no further rebirths.

Parvati

"Daughter of the mountain." Shiva's consort, in a serene form.

Pashupati

Shiva as "lord of the beasts." In South India, Shiva in this form has four arms: one hand is in an attitude of blessing, a second is open as if offering a boon, a third holds an axe, and from the last a small deer springs.

pata

A metal, stone, or earthenware plaque depicting the figure of a god.

pediment

The triangular upper portion of a wall above the portico.

phanom

Mountain. Used to name a temple, sanctuary, or sacred site.

phra

Sacred or holy; a title of respect used as a prefix for an ordained monk, venerated Buddha image, or object or member of the nobility.

Phra Narai

See **Narayana**.

Phra That

A relic of the Buddha or any chedi sheltering a relic of the Buddha. Also the chedis of northern Thailand used as funerary monu-

ments having a square base within which a
cubical cell contains ancestral ashes.

phreah
Khmer word for sacred.

pilaster
A column projecting slightly from the wall
usually found on each side of an open
doorway.

plinth
A square block at the base of a column or
pedestal; also a rectangular or circular base on
which a statue is placed.

pradakshina
Circumambulation around the temple,
keeping the shrine to the right, in a clockwise
direction.

Prajnaparamita
The bodhisattva of wisdom in Mahayana
Buddhism. She is usually seated on a lotus
throne and has four arms, the two lower ones
in the attitude of turning the Wheel of the
Law. Her attributes are a lotus and a book.
Having acquired the supreme virtue of wisdom, she is regarded as the spiritual mother
of all buddhas and the philosophical aspect
of Tara.

Prambanan
The greatest Hindu temple in Java, known
as Candi Prambanan. Located on the
Prambanan plain, it was built between 900

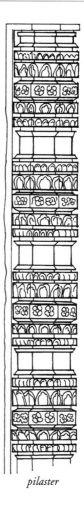

pilaster

and 930 C.E. The central tower rises almost vertically to 45 m. It was built as a symbolic re-creation of the cosmic Mt. Meru.

prana

The inner breath filling and expanding the body.

prang

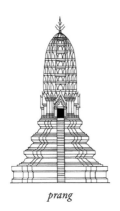

prang

A type of Thai chedi in the form of a tower and shaped like a corn cob with many tiers of cells. Based on the Khmer sanctuary tower, it is commonly found in the architecture of the Ayutthaya and Bangkok periods.

prasada

See **prasat**.

prasat

Palace for a king or god. In religious and secular architecture, the sanctuary tower represents Mt. Meru. In Thailand, prasat refers to the entire temple building. In Cambodia, the prasat hin, or stone palace, was popular.

prasavya

Procession around a temple keeping the shrine to the left.

Prithivi

See **Shiva**.

puja

Showing devotion to a god by worshiping its image.

pura
Balinese temple.

Purana
Ancient stories or legends written in the Gupta period based on pre-Hindu traditions. There are eight "Great Puranas" and many lesser ones.

Pyu
Early inhabitants of Burma.

Q

qabr
A Muslim grave.

qabristan
A Muslim tomb.

qibla
Direction for Muslim prayer.

qila
A fort.

quan
A place of Taoist worship.

quincunx
A square platform with five towers, one in each corner and one in the center.

Quran
See **Koran**.

R

Radha

Krishna's favorite love and playmate. She represents the human soul, and he the universal spirit.

Rahu

A demon depicted with a monster's head.

Rama

Rakshasa

A nocturnal demon of a malevolent nature who haunts cemeteries, animates dead bodies, and generally harasses human beings in a variety of ways. In the Ramayana, Ravana is chief of the Rakshasas.

Rama

The hero of the Indian epic, the Ramayana, and seventh avatara of Vishnu.

Ramakien

The Thai version of the Ramayana.

Ramayana

The Indian epic drama dated between 400 and 200 B.C.E. narrating the story of Rama and the abduction of his wife, Sita, by the demon king Ravana of Lanka, and the many battles to rescue her.

rasmi

Ray of light. The halo surrounding the head of the Buddha; the flame emanating from his ushnisha symbolizing the superior powers of the Buddha.

Ratnasambhava

"Jewel-born." In Mahayana Buddhism, the transcendental Buddha of the southern universe. He performs varadamudra, the gesture of charity.

Ravana

Demon king of Lanka who is the enemy of Lord Rama in the Ramayana epic; depicted with ten heads and twenty arms.

redented

A Thai architectural feature of pillars and chedis whereby the angle of each level is recessed from the one below.

redented chedi

reincarnation

The belief that after death the soul moves into another bodily form and continues to live.

reliquary

A container for a sacred relic, such as a chest, shrine, or casket.

rishi

A Hindu sage, ascetic, or hermit usually residing in the Himalayas. A holy person who received the revelation of the Vedic hymns. Often portrayed as a seated bearded figure with a headdress of bark.

rishi

Rudra

"Howler." The Vedic god whose many aspects are both beneficent and destructive. An early form of the Hindu god Shiva.

S

sadhu

One who renounces the secular world to follow a religious life.

Sa Huynh

The ancient culture located in the area of modern Vietnam considered to be the predecessor of Cham culture dating back about four thousand years.

Sailendra

"Lord of the mountain." A Mahayana Buddhist dynasty that ruled central Java during the 8th and 9th centuries C.E., and ruled Shrivijaya during the 8th and 13th centuries C.E.

Sakya

See **Shakya**.

Sakyamuni

See **Shakyamuni**.

sala

An open-sided pavilion usually found in the compound of a Buddhist monastery as a place of rest.

sal tree

The kind of tree under which the historical Buddha is believed to have been born.

samanera

An ascetic, mendicant, or wanderer of

various religious orders in ancient India. The term now refers to a novice in the Buddhist order.

sampot
A garment covering the lower part of the body, usually worn by male deities in Khmer art.

samsara
The transmigration of the soul through the endless cycle of birth, aging, death, and rebirth accompanied by suffering. Buddhists and Hindus try to find release from this cycle of reincarnation by striving to eliminate craving and desire.

Sanchi
Important Buddhist site on which the Great Stupa was built. The first stupa was built on this site by Emperor Ashoka in the 3rd century C.E. One hundred years later it was enlarged to twice the size.

Sangha
The community of monks following the precepts of Buddhism. Part of the Triple Gem, along with the Buddha and the Dharma.

Sanskrit
"Pure." An ancient language of India, of Indo-European derivation, used in the sacred texts of Hinduism and Buddhism.

sapan
Bridge, in Thai.

Sapta Matrikis

Seven divine mothers: Brahmi, Maheshvari, Vaishnavi, Kaumari, Indrani, Varahi, and Chamundi.

Sapta Sindhava

Seven great rivers, referred to in the Vedas: the Ganges, Jumna, Sarsuti, Satlej, Parushni, Marudvridha, and Arjikiya. Sometimes refers to the seven great oceans of the world.

Sarasvati

The Hindu goddess of learning and the arts, and Brahma's consort. In Mahayana Buddhism she is the goddess of teaching, music, and poetry, and the consort of Manjushri.

Sariputtra

One of the main disciples of the Buddha.

Sarnath

Location in North India near Varanasi where the Buddha preached his first sermon after his enlightenment.

Sawankhalok

A town in north-central Thailand famous for its ceramics, produced during and after the Sukhothai period, from the 14th to 16th centuries C.E.

sema

See **bai sema**.

Sena

A Hindu dynasty in eastern India of the 12th century C.E., following the Pala dynasty. Art style known as the Pala-Sena style.

Sesha

See **Shesha.**

Shaivite

Pertaining to Shiva; a Hindu who believes that Shiva is the supreme god.

shakti

The female consort of a Hindu god who personifies the god's divine energy or life force. For example, Parvati is the shakti of Shiva.

Shakya

The clan of Prince Siddhartha, who became the historical Buddha.

Shakyamuni

The sage of the Shakya clan, another name for the historical Buddha.

sheesh mahal

Palace apartment in India decorated with mirror work.

Shesha

The mythical snake with one thousand heads, a symbol of cosmic waters. The Hindu god Vishnu rests on Shesha during the time that separates two cosmic periods, a theme popular in the architectural decoration of

Southeast Asia. Also known as Ananta and Vasuki.

shikhara

The spire of a North Indian temple.

Shiva

Shiva

One of the three principal gods of Hinduism, representing the force of destruction as well as regenerative energy. In art he is shown with matted hair in a topknot, wearing a Brahmanical cord which is sometimes in the form of a serpent. He has a third eye on his forehead and a crescent moon in his hair. His many attributes include a trident and an axe. His consort is Devi (also known as Parvati and Uma). His mount is the bull Nandi.

Shivalinga

A phallic symbol representing the regenerative force of Shiva, worshiped in India and Southeast Asia.

Shri

The goddess of good fortune and wealth, the consort of the Hindu god Vishnu. Also known as Lakshmi.

Shrivijaya

A kingdom of the 8th to 13th century C.E. which extended over Sumatra and the Malay peninsula, including parts of present-day southern Thailand. Its extent and capital are still disputed. Also an art style.

Shudra

Caste of unskilled laborers in India, the lowest of the four Hindu castes.

Shwedagon

Great bell-shaped pagoda of Yangon, Burma, covered with sixty tons of gold leaf and encrusted with precious gems. Construction is said to have started in the 5th century C.E., to house eight sacred hairs of the Buddha. It has remained in continuous use, and has been enlarged, restored, and rebuilt over the centuries.

Siam

The historical name of Thailand until 1939.

Siddhartha

"Goal reached." The given name of the prince who later became the historical Buddha.

Siddhatta

See **Siddhartha**.

Sikhism

An Indian religion founded by Nanak in the late 15th century placing importance on surrender to God and service to people. Sikhs share the Hindu beliefs of karma and rebirth, but reject the rituals. There have been ten great gurus or teachers in Sikhism.

sim

Main sanctuary or ordination hall in a Laotian Buddhist temple.

simha

simha

Lion, usually depicted in mythical form in art.

simhamukha

Lion-face or mask, often seen in Indian and Khmer temples as architectural decoration. In a stylized form it is also known as kirtimukha or kala.

simhasana

A lion-throne.

singha

See **simha**.

Sita

Wife of Rama and the embodiment of feminine virtues, heroine of the Indian Ramayana and Thai Ramakien epic poems.

Siva

See **Shiva**.

Skanda

The god of war, whose mount is a peacock. One of the sons of Shiva and his consort.

soma, Soma

The nectar of immortality or amrita. Also another name of Chandra, the moon god.

spean

Bridge, in Khmer.

srah

Pond, in Khmer.

Sravasti

An ancient city in North India where the Buddha meditated and performed a series of miracles. In the great miracle, in response to those who doubted his teaching, the Buddha levitated while flames and water gushed from his body, and his image multiplied.

srei

Woman, in Khmer, as in Banteay Srei.

Sri

See **Shri**.

Srivijaya

See **Shrivijaya**.

stambha

Free-standing column.

stele

Inscribed stone panel or slab, the earliest method of recording historical events.

Sthaviravada

See **Theravada**.

stucco

A type of plaster used in architectural decoration, sculpture, and as mortar between bricks.

stupa

Mound. Term used in India for the mound-shaped structure sheltering the relics of the historical Buddha or revered monks. Sometimes houses holy objects. Also known as a chedi.

stupa

Subramanya

See **Skanda**.

Suchada

See **Sujata**.

Suddhodana

Father of the historical Buddha and ruler of Kapilavastu, now located in Nepal.

Sudra

See **Shudra**.

Sufi

An Islamic mystic.

Sujata

The pious woman who gave Gautama, the would-be Buddha, the meal that broke his fast before his enlightenment.

Sukhavati

The western heaven of Mahayana Buddhism presided over by Amitabha, one of the transcendental buddhas.

Sukhothai

A contemporary Thai city and the kingdom in central Thailand during the 13th to 14th centuries C.E. Also the name of the art style produced during that period. A major artistic innovation of this art period was the walking Buddha image.

Surya

The sun god, represented with a halo and a

Sukhothai Buddha image

lotus in each hand. He rides a chariot drawn
by seven horses.

sutra

Thread. The teachings or discourses of the
Buddha which form the second part of the
Buddhist canon, the Tripitaka. Also used for
certain Hindu texts.

sutta

See **sutra**.

Surya

Suvarnabhumi

"Land of gold." In ancient literature it
referred to an area in Southeast Asia, possibly
Thailand.

swastika

Well being. An auspicious emblem, shaped
like an equal-armed cross with bent ends. In
Buddhism, interpreted as a symbol of the
dharmachakra, the Wheel of the Law.

swastika

T

Ta Keo

"Tower of crystal." Shaivite temple located
in Angkor, built by Jayavarman V in the late
10th and early 11th centuries C.E.

Taj Mahal

A mausoleum built in the 17th century by
the Mughal emperor Shah Jahan in memory
of his wife. It is located on the bank of the
Yamuna River in Agra, North India. Built

entirely of marble, it represents a fusion of Indian and Persian styles to create a distinct architectural form.

tandava

The cosmic dance of the Hindu god Shiva.

tanka

See **thangka**.

Tantima

Mythical bird holding a staff, usually found in pairs serving as guardians at temple entrances in Thailand.

tantra

A group of sacred texts and the practices associated with them in Tibetan Buddhism. There are also tantric texts in Hinduism. The central theme of tantra is the divine energy and creative power represented by the feminine aspect of a god, personified as a goddess.

Tantric Buddhism

A type of Vajrayana Buddhism important in northeastern India after the 8th century C.E., and still surviving in Nepal, Tibet, and Mongolia. It expanded the Buddhist pantheon, and placed a greater importance on esoteric practices based on the tantra.

Taoism

An influential philosophy in China, founded by Lao Tzu probably in the 4th century B.C.E. Tao-te Ching or "The Book of the Way" is attributed to Lao-tzu and is the basis of philosophical Taoism. Tao is the all-embracing, ultimate, and primordial principle. The goal is to become one with the Tao by realizing the universal law of the return of everything to its source.

Tara

"One who enables to cross-over;" the savioress. Vajrayana Buddhism has five goddesses called Tara, corresponding to the five jinas or transcendental buddhas. They are the consorts of the five great bodhisattvas, who were created by the jinas and have the rank of bodhisattva in the hierarchy. In Tibetan Buddhism there are twenty-one forms of Tara, each having a different color, posture, and attribute. They can have either peaceful or wrathful appearances. The most frequently seen forms are Green Tara and White Tara.

Tavatimsa

The heaven of thirty-three gods, presided over by Indra, and one of the heavens which can be reached by accumulated merit. The Buddha spent one rainy season in this heaven preaching to his mother who had died shortly after his birth. The Buddha descending from Tavatimsa heaven is a common scene in temple murals in Southeast Asia.

tazaung

Small pavilions found within Buddhist temple complexes in Burma.

Taxila

An ancient Buddhist center of learning, now in ruins in present-day Pakistan.

tham
Cave, in Thai.

thangka
Cloth, often silk, painted with Tibetan Mahayana deities; also an object of veneration and inspiration for meditation.

terra cotta
Hard, brownish-orange clay used for architectural decoration, figurines, and pottery.

that
Shrine housing Buddhist relics commemorating the Buddha's life, or a funerary temple for royalty. Peculiar to Laos and parts of Thailand.

thein
The ordination hall in Buddhist temple compounds in Burma.

thep
See **deva**.

thepchumnum
The rows of devas, Garudas, or yakshas in the posture of adoration or worship, often adorning Thai temples in mural or sculptural form.

thephanom
The figure of a deva or devi in a worshiping gesture in Thai art.

thephanom

Theravada

"Words of the elders" or "teachings of the elders." A Hinayana sect that spread from India to Sri Lanka and Southeast Asia, where it is the dominant form of Buddhism. Its texts are written in the Pali language.

thom

Large or great, in Khmer, as in "Angkor Thom."

thongkham-plae

See **gold leaf**.

Thorani

The earth-mother who appears as a witness to the Buddha's accumulated merit just before the moment of his enlightenment. In art, she is often depicted as wringing water from her hair. "Calling the earth (mother) to witness" is a popular hand gesture in Buddhist iconography. See **bhumisparsamudra**.

tie beam

A horizontal beam connecting the lower ends of two opposite principal rafters, forming the base of a roof truss.

Tipitaka

See **Tripitaka**.

Tirthankara

The twenty-four sages or great teachers in the Jain religion.

Thorani

Totsakan

torana

A gateway of a temple, stupa, or palace in North India, often with elaborate lintels.

Totsachat

The name given in Thai to the stories of the last ten lives of the Buddha, before his birth as Prince Siddhartha. Part of the Jatakas.

Totsakan

The Thai name of the ten-headed demon king who abducts Sita, the wife of Rama, in the epic Ramakien. Known as Ravana in the Ramayana.

trilok

See **triphum**.

triphum

Three worlds. Refers to the three realms of Buddhist cosmology, viz. heaven, earth, and hell, depicted in murals and in the symbolism of the stupa.

Traipitok

See **Tripitaka**.

trairat

See **triratna**.

trakien

Time period, in Vietnamese.

Tra-kieu

Art style of Champa dated from the second

half of the 9th century to the end of the 10th
century when its capital was Indrapura in the
north of the kingdom.

tribhanga
Triple flexion. A posture in dance, sculpture, and painting in which the body is
curved with the right hip thrust out forming
an S-shape.

trigram
Symbol indicating the eight points of the
compass used by geomancers. Each trigram
consists of a different combination of three
lines. The lines may be broken in the middle
(yin) or unbroken (yang). When used for
divination, trigrams are arranged in a circle
with yin and yang signs in the middle. Seen
as a decorative motif on ceramics, buildings,
and textiles.

trigram

Trilokyavijaya
"Conqueror of the three worlds." The
name of a divinity of terrifying appearance in
Tantric Buddhism depicted with four faces,
eight hands, and sometimes wearing a garland
of small Buddha images. It is also one of the
major Mahayana bodhisattvas.

Trimurti
"Three aspects." Term used for the Hindu
divine triad: Brahma, Vishnu, and Shiva, and
most commonly associated with the image
which represents three aspects of Shiva at
Elephanta, in India.

trisula

Tripitaka

"Three baskets." The name for the palm-leaf manuscripts containing the three sections of Theravada Buddhist scriptures in the Pali language.

Triratana

The Triple Gem, the three objects of devotion for all Buddhists: the historical Buddha; the Dharma, or the teaching; and the Sangha, or the brotherhood of monks. Represented in Buddhist temples by the three prongs of a trident.

trisula

Trident, weapon of the Hindu god Shiva, sometimes used as his symbol.

tumpal

Triangular motif at the end of a handwoven fabric in Thailand.

Tushita

One of the highest heavens in Buddhist cosmology. The heaven where the historical Buddha resided before being born as Prince Siddhartha, and the heaven of the future Buddha, Maitreya.

Tusita

See **Tushita**.

tympanum

See **gable board**.

U

ubosot
In Thailand, the building in a Buddhist temple compound where religious ceremonies such as ordination take place. Originally the term referred to certain days of fasting. Abbreviated as bot.

Ucchaisaravas
The white horse of Indra created during the churning of the ocean.

Uma
One of the names of the consort of the Hindu god Shiva. Also known as Parvati.

Umamahesvara
Image of Shiva and Uma together, sometimes riding the bull Nandi.

Umamahesvara

Umapati
Uma's husband Shiva.

unna
See **urna**.

Upanishads
Philosophical treatises of Hinduism developed during the 8th to 6th centuries B.C.E., which became part of Vedic literature.

upasaka
Buddhist lay people who shave their heads like monks, but dress in white. Although not fully ordained, in Theravada Buddhist coun-

urna

tries they vow to abide by certain precepts and live in monasteries. The female form is upasika.

Upendra
   Title given to Krishna by Indra.

uposatha
   See **ubosot**.

urna
   Whorl of hair between the eyebrows of the Buddha, representing the third eye of great wisdom, one of the signs of an enlightened being. Often indicated as a round mark.

ushnisha
   In Buddhist iconography, a protuberance or topknot on the head of the Buddha, one of the marks of an enlightened being.

ushnisha: five variations

U-Thong
   A town in western Thailand that flourished during the 12th to 15th centuries C.E. Also the art style of Buddha images produced in that period.

V

vahana
Vehicle or mount of a god. For example, the mount of Vishnu is Garuda.

Vairochana
See **Mahavairochana**.

Vaishnava
Worshiper of Vishnu, or those who consider Vishnu to be the principal god. Followers of this sect may be identified by an elongated U-shaped mark on their forehead.

Vaishya
The third of the four major Hindu castes, whose members engage in commerce.

vajra
Thunderbolt or diamond implying indestructibility. Principal symbol of Vajrayana Buddhism representing absolute truth. In Hinduism, the thunderbolt is wielded by several gods, including Indra.

Vajradhara
"The wielder of the diamond or thunder-bolt," a representation of Adi-Buddha, usually shown crowned and bejeweled. In Nepal and Tibet, he is shown with his female counterpart. In Khmer art, he holds a vajra and a bell with hands crossed over his chest.

vajra

Vajrapani

"The bearer of the diamond or the thunderbolt," a bodhisattva in Vajrayana Buddhism. He holds a vajra, or sometimes two lotuses supported by a bell and a vajra. In Mahayana Buddhism he is sometimes considered to be Avalokitesvara.

Vajrasana

A diamond throne. Also a posture seen in Buddhist and Hindu iconography. The legs are bent and crossed with feet resting on opposite thighs, soles upward.

Vajrasattva

"The one whose essence is the diamond or thunderbolt." In Vajrayana Buddhism, he is the principle of purity and purification and his role is similar to that of Vajradhara. In Khmer art, he holds a vajra against his chest and a bell against his left hip.

Vajrayana

"The diamond vehicle." A branch of Mahayana Buddhism which began in the 4th century C.E. It was important in Northeast India, from which it spread to Nepal and Tibet, and East Asia. It promoted highly developed ritual worship practices using mantra or mystical incantation, mandalas, or magical diagrams, and yoga, and union with the universal spirit. Also known as Mantrayana.

Vamana

"Midget." One of the avataras or descents

of Vishnu in the form of a midget.

Vanaspati
"Lord of the jungle," in Hindu mythology.
See **Panaspati**.

Van Mieu
Temple of literature which honors the cult
of Confucius. Temples were built in the
capitals of Hanoi and Hue in Vietnam.

Varaha
"Boar." One of the avataras or descents of
Vishnu in the form of a boar.

varamudra
In Buddhist iconography, the gesture of
bestowing favor, with right arm extended,
palm upward, and left arm pendant.

Vardhamana
Founder of the Jain religion later know as
Mahavir, the great hero. He was born into a
royal family probably in 599 B.C.E. in the
same region of North India as the Buddha.
He traveled and preached for thirty years and
died at the age of seventy-two, in 527 B.C.E.

varman
"Protected by." A title used by various
rulers, particularly Khmer kings.

varna
Class or caste. The four castes of Hinduism
are: Brahman, the learned class; Kshatriya,
the royal or warrior class; Vaishya, the trading

class; and Shudra, the agricultural and service class.

Varuna

The Vedic god of the waters and protector of the western direction. His mount is the makara or crocodile.

Vasudeva

Father of Krishna.

Vasuki

King of the serpents or nagas who was used as the churning rope when the ocean was churned by the gods and the demons to retrieve the nectar of immortality. Also known as Ananta and Shesha.

vat

Temple, in Khmer.

Vayu

The Vedic god of wind or air, and guardian of the northwest direction. His mount is an antelope.

Veda

"Knowledge." Refers to a collection of very ancient hymns and verses sacred to Hinduism. The earliest was composed between 1500 and 1200 B.C.E. There are four Vedas: Rig, Sama, Yajur, and Atharva.

vedika

A railing enclosing a chaitya or an object of veneration.

Vesara

A style of temple architecture of the Deccan area in India.

Vessantara

See **Vishvantara**.

vihan

See **vihara**.

vihara

Originally the dwelling place of Buddhist monks. In Thailand, it refers to a hall in the temple compound where religious services are held. It may or may not house a Buddha image.

Vijayanagara

A powerful kingdom in south-central India in the 15th and 16th centuries C.E. Also an art style. Its capital city was Hampi.

vimana

A car or chariot of the gods, also the towered shrine of Hindu temples in the South Indian style.

Vinaya

The first of the three-part Buddhist scripture, the Tripitaka. The Vinaya lists all the rules of discipline.

virasana

The posture of the hero. A sitting posture often seen in iconography in which the right foot rests on the left thigh, with the left foot under the right thigh.

Vishnu

vitarkamudra

votive tablet

Vishnu

One of the principal gods of Hinduism, the preserver of the universe, depicted as seated, standing, or reclining on a serpent on the cosmic sea. Often shown with four arms holding a conch, a lotus, a wheel, and a club. When the forces of evil become too strong, he descends to earth assuming different forms to restore the balance. There have been nine of these avataras; the tenth is yet to come.

Vishvantara

One of the Jatakas, the last of the previous lives of the historical Buddha. It teaches the virtue of charity.

vitarkamudra

A hand gesture of the Buddha indicating exposition. The right arm is bent, the index or ring finger touching the thumb, palm outward. Sometimes seen with both hands performing the same gesture.

votive tablet

A religious tablet or plaque made to express a wish or prayer, or made to express the fulfillment of a vow.

W

wat

Buddhist monasteries in Thailand and Laos, encompassing buildings used for religious, educational, and residential purposes.

wayang

Puppets made of many different materials in Indonesia.

Wheel of the Law

Iconographic symbol of the Dharma, the teachings of the Buddha, which are eternal. See **dharmachakra**.

Y

yabyum

The concept of the unity of the masculine principle and the feminine principle in Vajrayana Buddhism. In Tibetan art, depicted as masculine and feminine deities in sexual union.

yakshas

Mythical beings, nature spirits. In India, guardians of the wealth of the gods. In Southeast Asia, guardians of temples. They look fierce, but are believed to be benign. The feminine form is yakshi.

yali

A horned lion, used in architectural decorations in Indian temples.

Yama

The Vedic god of death. The judge of the dead, guardian of the southern direction. His mount is a buffalo.

Yamuna

River in North India, and the name of the goddess personifying the river.

yantra

Magical geometric diagram, usually square, used in meditation, especially in Vajrayana and Tantric Buddhism. A mandala is a type of yantra.

Yashoda

The foster mother of Krishna, who was an incarnation of Vishnu. In Indian art a popular theme is Yashoda with the child Krishna.

Yashodhara

The wife of Prince Siddhartha, also known as Gopa.

yin-yang

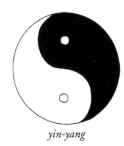

yin-yang

Two polar energies that cause the universe in Taoist belief. Yin represents the feminine, the passive, the dark, and the soft; yang represents the masculine, the active, the bright, and the hard. Yin is symbolized as the moon, water, the color black, and the direction north; yang is symbolized as the sun, fire, the color red, and the direction south. Represented in the popular symbol of a circle divided into two curved halves, one white and one black.

yoga

To unite. A system of physical, mental, and spiritual discipline, the ultimate aim of which is to unite with the universal spirit.

yogi

One who practices yoga. The feminine form is yogin.

yoni

An object of worship symbolic of female creative energy, represented as the female sex organ, in the form of a square pedestal with hollow top, and a trough at one end. When in combination with a lingam or phallic representation of Shiva's creative force, it symbolizes creation.

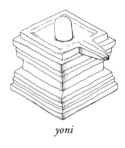

yoni

yuga

Time period in Indian cosmology. There are four yugas: Krita or Satya, Treta, Dvapara, and Kali, in descending order of righteousness. The present period is Kali yuga.

Z

zari

The cenotaph in an Islamic tomb.

zat

Classical Burmese drama, usually based on the Ramayana.

zayat

Prayer pavilions in Buddhist temple complexes in Burma.

zedi

Burmese word for chedi.

Zen

The Japanese term for a school of Mahayana Buddhism. Known as Ch'an in Chinese and Dhyana in Sanskrit, Zen places emphasis on self-realization and discourages ritual practices.

zenana

Segregated apartment for women practicing purdah, seen in Indian palaces.

ziarat

A holy Islamic tomb.

SELECT READING

GENERAL

Fisher, Robert E. *Buddhist Art and Architecture*. Singapore: Thames and Hudson, 1993.

Hall, D. G. E. *A History of South-East Asia*. London: Macmillan, 1981.

Lewis, Bernard, ed. *The World of Islam*. London: Thames and Hudson, 1992.

Rawson, Philip. *The Art of Southeast Asia*. London: Thames and Hudson, 1993.

Rowland, Benjamin. *The Pelican History of Art*. Baltimore, Md.: Penguin Books, 1970.

Sen, K. M. *Hinduism*. Baltimore, Md.: Penguin Books, 1987.

Sherman, Lee E. *A History of Far Eastern Art*. London: Thames and Hudson, 1978.

BURMA

Fraser-Lu, Sylvia. *Burmese Crafts Past and Present*. New York: Oxford University Press, 1994.

Griswold, Alexander, B. *Art of Burma, Korea and Tibet*. New York: Crown Publications, 1964.

CAMBODIA

Chandler, David P. *A History of Cambodia*. 2nd ed. Chiang Mai, Thailand: Silkworm Books, 1993.

Jacques, Claude, and Michael Freeman. *Angkor Cities and Temples*. Bangkok: River Books, 1997.

Moore, Elizabeth, and Siribhadra Smitthi. *Palaces of the Gods*. Bangkok: River Books, 1992.

Rooney, D. F. *Angkor, An Introduction to the Temples*. Bangkok: Asia Books, 1994.

Roveda, Vittorio. *Khmer Mythology*. Bangkok: River Books, 1997.

Mabett, Ian, and David Chandler. *The Khmers*. Oxford: Blackwell Publishers, 1995.

INDIA

Blurton, Richard T. *Hindu Art*. London: British Museum Press, 1992.

Craven, Roy C. *Indian Art, A Concise History*. London: Thames and Hudson, 1991.

Huntington, Susan. *The Art of Ancient India*. Tokyo: Weatherhill,1985.

Davies, Philip. *The Penguin Guide to the Monuments of India,Vol. II*. Baltimore, Md.: Penguin Books, 1989.

Watson, Francis. *A Concise History of India*. London: Thames and Hudson, 1987.

INDONESIA

Miksic, John. *Borobudur, Golden Tales of the Buddhas*. Berkeley, Calif.: Periphus Editions, 1990.

Dumarcay, Jacques. *The Temples of Java*. Singapore: Oxford University Press, 1986.

Dumarcay, Jacques. *Borobudur*. Kuala Lumpur: Oxford University Press, 1979.

THAILAND

Boisselier, Jean. *The Heritage of Thai Sculpture*. Bangkok: Asia Books, 1987.

Diskul, S. *Art in Thailand: A Brief History*. Bangkok: Amarin Press, 1986.

Fickle, Dorothy. *Images of the Buddha in Thailand*. Singapore: Oxford University Press, 1989.

Krairiksh, Piriya. *Art in Peninsular Thailand Pior to the Fourteenth Century A.D.* Bangkok: Fine Arts Department, 1980.

Ringis, Rita. *Thai Temples and Temple Murals*. Kuala Lumpur: Oxford University Press, 1990.

Stratton, Carol, and Miriam McNair Scott. *Art of Sukhothai*. Kuala Lumpur: Oxford University Press, 1981.

VIETNAM

Nguyen, Tran and Le. *The Celebrated Pagodas of Hue*. Hanoi: Writers Association Publishing House, 1993.

Pham, Huy Thong. *Cham Sculpture*. Hanoi: Social Sciences Publishing House, 1988.

Phan Huy My. *Champa Collection*. Ho Chi Minh: Viet Nam Historical Museum, 1994.

Tran Ky Phuong. *Cham Ruins: Journey in Search of An Ancient Civilization*. Hanoi: Gioi Publishers, 1993.
Vo Van Tuong. *Vietnam's Famous Pagodas*. Hanoi, 1994

SUGGESTED MUSEUMS

BURMA
State Museum, Mandalay
Archaeological Museum, Pagan
Museum of the International Library for Advanced Buddhist Studies, Rangoon
National Museum, Rangoon

CAMBODIA
Archaeological Repository of Angkor, Angkor (Siem Reap)
Musee Nationale du Cambodge, Phnom Penh
Museum of Wat Po Veal, Battambang

FRANCE
Guimet Museum, Paris

INDIA
Archaeological Museum, Mathura
Archaeological Museum, Nalanda
Archaeological Museum, Sarnath
Indian Museum, Calcutta
National Museum of India, New Delhi
Patna Museum, Patna
Prince of Wales Museum of Western India, Bombay
Salar Jung Museum, Hyderabad

INDONESIA
Archaeological Institute of Indonesia, Jakarta
Archaeological Institute, Prambanan

LAOS
Royal Palace, National Museum, Luang Prabang
Wat Vixun Collection, Luang Prabang
Wat Phra Keo Collection, Vientiane
Wat Sisakhet Collection, Vientiane

NETHERLANDS
Museum van Azlatische Kunst, Amsterdam
Koninklijk Instituut voor de Tropen, Amsterdam

THAILAND
National Museum, Ayutthaya
National Museum, Bangkok
National Museum, Chiang Saen
National Museum, Lamphun
National Museum, Nakhon Si Thammarat
National Museum, Phimai

UNITED KINGDOM
British Museum, London
Victoria and Albert Museum, London

UNITED STATES
Boston Museum of Fine Arts
Los Angeles County Museum
Metropolitan Museum of Art, New York
Nelson Atkins Museum, Kansas City
Asian Art Museum of San Francisco

VIETNAM
Museum of Cham Sculpture, Da Nang
Historical Museum of Vietnam, Hanoi
Musee Khai-dinh, Hue
History Museum, Ho Chi Minh